READING
with
UNDERSTANDING
a comprehension course

JOHN SEELY

OXFORD UNIVERSITY PRESS

Oxford University Press, Walton Street, Oxford OX2 6DP

Oxford   New York   Toronto
Delhi   Bombay   Calcutta   Madras   Karachi
Petaling Jaya   Singapore   Hong Kong   Tokyo
Nairobi   Dar es Salaam   Cape Town
Melbourne   Auckland

and associated companies in
Berlin   Ibadan

Oxford is a trade mark of Oxford University Press

© Oxford University Press 1983

ISBN 0 19 831141 9

First published 1983
Reprinted 1984, 1985, 1989, 1991

Also by John Seely:

Oxford Secondary English

Book 1   0 19 831133 8   Teacher's Book 1   0 19 831134 6
Book 2   0 19 831135 4   Teacher's Book 2   0 19 831136 2
Book 3   0 19 831137 0   Teacher's Book 3   0 19 831138 9

Dramakit   0 19 913238 0

Playkits   0 19 913259 3

In Context   0 19 913222 4

Typeset in Great Britain by
Rowland Phototypesetting Ltd, Bury St Edmunds, Suffolk
Printed in Hong Kong

CONTENTS

1   BEST IN THE BUSINESS   *Betsy Byars*   5

2   DISARMING A MINE   *Cleodie Mackinnon*   10

3   FAMOUS DOCTORS   *Gareth Stevens*   14

4   AIR RAID   *Robert Westall*   19

5   MARCH TO SAFETY   *Alan Burgess*   24

6   THE LABOURS OF HERCULES   *Rex Warner*   30

7   THE CAVES   *Lionel Davidson*   34

8   THE SPIRE   *Alan Garner*   38

9   SIEGE   *Geoffrey Hindley*   43

10   THE WILD WEST   *Kenneth Ulyatt*   48

11   CHUNNY'S PIG   *John Griffin*   52

12   KILL TO EAT   *Kath Walker*   57

13   FIRE   *Ivan Southall*   63

14   THE ANT WAR   *Gerald Durrell*   68

15   HUNTERS AND HUNTED   *David Attenborough & Jane Burton*   73

16   SEARCHING FOR WATER   *Andrew Salkey*   80

17   BREAD   *Carolyn Meyer*   86

18   MILITARY TRAINING   *Peter Dickinson*   92

19   THE MOONPATH   *Robert E. Swindells*   97

WHAT HAPPENS NEXT?   103

ACKNOWLEDGEMENTS

The publishers would like to thank the following for permission to reprint copyright material.

David Attenborough: 'Hunters and Hunted' from *Life on Earth* (1980). Reprinted by permission of William Collins Sons & Co. Ltd. **Alan Burgess**: 'March to Safety' adapted from *The Small Woman* (1957). Reprinted by permission of Evans Brothers Ltd. **Jane Burton**: 'Hunters and Hunted' from *Animals of the African Year* (1972). Reprinted by permission of the author and Eurobook Ltd. **Betsy Byars**: 'Best in the Business' adapted from *Winged Colt of Casa Mia* (1973). Reprinted by permission of The Bodley Head. **Arthur C. Clarke**: 'Security Check' from *Of Time and Stars* (Gollancz 1972). Reprinted by permission of David Higham Associates Ltd. **Lionel Davidson**: 'The Caves' adapted from *Under Plum Lake* (Cape 1980). Copyright © 1980 by Manningford Limited. Reprinted by permission of Anthony Sheil Associates Ltd. **Peter Dickinson**: 'Military Training' from *City of Gold and Other Stories from the Old Testament* (1980) Reprinted by permission of Victor Gollancz Ltd. **Gerald Durrell**: 'The Ant War' adapted from *Encounters with Animals* (1958). Reprinted by permission of Granada Publishing Ltd. **Alan Garner**: 'The Spire' from *The Stone Book*. Copyright © Alan Garner 1976. Reprinted by permission of Collins Publishers. **John Griffin**: 'Chunny's Pig' adapted from *Skulker Wheat and Other Stories* (1977). Reprinted by permission of William Heinemann Ltd. **Geoffrey Hindley**: 'Siege' adapted from *Under Siege* (1979). Reprinted by permission of Angus & Robertson (UK) Ltd. **Shirley Jackson**: 'Charles' from *The Lottery and other stories*. Reprinted by permission of A. M. Heathe & Co., Ltd., on behalf of the estate of the late Shirley Jackson. **Cleodie MacKinnon**: 'Disarming a mine' from *Stories of Courage*. Copyright © OUP 1967. Reprinted by permission of Oxford University Press. **Carolyn Meyer**: from *The Bread Book*, Copyright © 1971 by Carolyn Meyer. Reprinted by permission of Joan Daves. **Bill Naughton**: 'A Good Six Penn'orth' from *The Goalkeeper's Revenge* (1961). Reprinted by permission of Harrap Ltd. **Richard Parker**: from *The Wheelbarrow Boy*, © 1953 by Mercury Press, Inc., from *The Magazine of Fantasy and Science Fiction*. Reprinted by permission of Curtis Brown Ltd., London. **Hans Peter Richter**: from *Friedrich* (Kestrel Books, 1975). Copyright © 1961 by Sebaldus-Verlag G.m.b.h., Nurnberg; © 1970 by Holt, Rinehart and Winston, Inc. Reprinted by permission of Penguin Books Ltd. **Andrew Salkey**: 'Searching for water' adapted from *Drought*. Copyright © OUP 1966. Reprinted by permission of Oxford University Press. **Ivan Southall**: 'Fire' adapted from *Ash Road* (1966). Reprinted by permission of Angus & Robertson (UK) Ltd. **Gareth Stevens**: 'Famous Doctors' adapted from *Famous Names in Medicine* (1978). Reprinted by permission of Wayland Publishers Ltd. **Robert E. Swindells**: from *The Moonpath and Other Stories* (1979). Reprinted by permission of A. Wheaton & Co., Ltd. **Kenneth Ulyatt**: 'The Wild West' adapted from *Outlaws* (Puffin Books, 1978). Copyright © Kenneth Ulyatt 1976. Reprinted by permission of Penguin Books Ltd. **Kath Walker**: 'Kill to Eat' adapted from *Stradbroke Dreamtime* (1972). Reprinted by permission of Angus & Robertson (UK) Ltd. **R. Westall**: 'Air Raid' adapted from *The Machine Gunners* (1975). Reprinted by permission of Macmillan, London & Basingstoke. **Rex Warner**: 'The Labours of Hercules' from *Men and Gods*. Reprinted by permission of Granada Publishing Ltd.

Every effort has been made to trace and contact copyright holders but this has not always been possible. We apologize for any infringement of copyright.

The Anglo-Chinese Institute, p. 24; Australian Information Service, p. 57; Anne Bolt, p. 80; J. Allan Cash, pp. 34, 97; Ronald Grant, p. 5; Imperial War Museum, pp. 10, 19; The Mansell Collection, p. 30; Popperfoto, p. 43; James Smith/Museum of English Rural Life, Reading, p. 52; J. Thomas, pp. 38, 92; John Topham Picture Library, p. 68; U.S. Forest Service, p. 48; The Wellcome Trustees, p. 14.

Illustrations by: Priscilla Barrett, Karen Dawes

1 BEST IN THE BUSINESS

Section A   Meeting

In this section twelve words have been missed out. The words are listed at the end of the passage.

☐ Read the passage carefully and try to work out which word should go in which space.

☐ Write the numbers of the spaces.

☐ Against each number write the word you have chosen.

We stood at the railroad station and —1— across the tracks at each other. He was a boy in a dark suit with his hair combed down —2—. He was holding a *Mad* magazine. I was a man in dusty boots and dusty pants with a —3— down the side of my face that no amount of dust could hide.

    I said, 'Charles?'

    He said, 'Uncle Coot? Is that you?'

'Yes.'

He tried to —4—. 'Well, it's me too.'

We kept standing there and then I stepped over to his side of the tracks. Charles was looking up at me, and for a second I could see the Texas sky —5— in his eyeglasses, the big white clouds. He cleared his throat and said, 'I —6— you heard I was coming.' He started rolling and unrolling his magazine. 'Or you wouldn't be here.'

'I got your mom's telegram this morning.'

'Well, she'll probably send for me in a few weeks or something,' he said. 'I won't be here for ever.' He made a tight —7— of the *Mad* magazine and held it in his fist.

'Well, sure,' I said. 'She'll send for you.' We stood there a minute more, and then I said, 'We might as well stop standing —8— and get in the truck.' We both tried to pick up his suitcase at the same time. Then I got it and carried it over to the truck and we got in.

We drove out of Martha and neither of us said anything for a mile or two. My truck's old and makes a lot of —9—, but it seemed quiet this morning. Once I cleared my throat, and he snapped his head around and asked, 'Did you say something?'

'I was just —10— my throat.'

'Oh, I thought you said something.'

'No.' I probably would have said something if I could have thought of anything to say, but I couldn't. We —11— on for a few more miles. I was looking straight ahead at the road. He was look-ing out the window at the Mountains. We passed a —12— called Devil's Back.

I said, 'I reckon this is different from back east where you were in school.'

'Yes.'

*flat   around   rode   grin   roll   looked   peak   scar   guess   noise
mirrored   clearing*

Section B   Cotton

In this section six sentences, or parts of sentences, have been missed out.

☐ Read the passage carefully.

☐ Try to work out what has been missed out.

☐ Write the number of each blank and beside it write what you think has

6

been missed out.

We drove another mile or two and then he said suddenly, '————
————————————1————————————.'
  I said, 'What?' because he had spoken real quiet.
  He turned his head toward me. 'I've seen you in the *movies*.'
  'Oh.'
  There was another silence, and then he said, 'I especially remember you in a movie called *Desert Flame*.'
  '————————————2————————————,' I said. Up until
this spring I had been in California doing stunts for western movies. I
had been doing stunts – or gags, as we call them – the biggest part of
my life and I can tell you that the stunts you see in the movies are real
and they are dangerous. There are tricks, of course – fences and barn
doors made of soft balsa wood to break easily, ground that's been dug
up and softened, rubber hose stirrups – but most of the horse stunts
you see are not faked, and stunt horses have to be special animals.
  Charles said, 'You were riding a white horse.'
  I said, 'Yeah.' Then I added again, 'But that's over now.' I wanted
the conversation to end.
  '————————————3————————————?'
  'Yeah.'
  'What was his name?'
  'Cotton.' There's a phrase stunt men have about horses – 'the best
in the business' – and that suited Cotton. In a stunt horse tempera-
ment is the important thing, not looks, and I had found Cotton on his
way to the slaughterhouse because of a badly wounded leg. ————
————————————4————————————. First I let him fall in a saw-
dust pit so he would get used to it, then I got him to fall when he was
walking, then trotting, and finally to fall in a full gallop, a beautiful fall
you've probably seen in a dozen movies.
  Maybe you remember the movie *Desert Flame* that Charles was
talking about and the scene where the white stallion falls in the
desert. ————————————5————————————. I rode Cot-
ton right to the top of the dune, reared him, pretended to take a shot
in the shoulder, fell backwards, and me and him rolled head over
hoof all the way down that dune without bruising either one of us.
Stunt men still talk about that fall sometimes.
  '————————————6————————————?' Charles asked.
'I'd like to see him.'
  'No, I don't have him any more.'
  'What happened?'
  I didn't answer.
  'What *happened*?' he asked again.
  I said, 'Nothing,' and began to drive a little faster.

Section C The accident

☐ Read the passage carefully and then answer the questions that follow.

What happened was something I couldn't talk about. That spring Cotton and I had been taking a fall for a movie called *Bright Glory*. The fall wasn't anything special, just a battle scene, and we were to come towards the camera in a full gallop and drop just before we got there. It wasn't anything unusual. Cotton and I had taken that same fall dozens of times with neither of us the worse for it. But this one fall my timing was off. It wasn't off more than a second, but we went down – not in the soft drop area but beyond it – and crashed into the camera. I got up but Cotton didn't: his front legs were broken.

It took something out of me. Cotton and I had been together for twelve years, and when I knew he was going to have to be shot – I knew it right when I scrambled to my feet in the dust and he didn't – well, I decided then that I wanted to go back home to Texas. The land called me. I wanted to look at the mountains again, to ride through the valleys, to have that bright blinding sky over me. I wanted to be by myself.

The whole thing came back to me as Charles was talking – the accident, the blood from my cheek falling on Cotton's white neck, the pistol shot. I reached up and rubbed the scar on my cheek.

Charles was still talking a mile a minute. 'And I remember you jumping across a cliff in *Thunder in Oklahoma*. Remember? You almost didn't make it, and you and the horse just hung there practically on the side of the cliff for a moment.'

'Yeah.'

'I stayed to see that part of the movie five times and it got better and better. Everybody in the audience held their breath, and some little kids down in the front screamed. Was the horse Cotton?'

I nodded.

'I told everybody that was my uncle up there on the screen – the lady selling popcorn, the man on the aisle, everybody. I don't think half of them believed me. It was the greatest thing I ever saw.'

'It wasn't that great, Charles. The cliff wasn't as high as it looked – they had the camera set at an angle so that it looked higher and –' I hesitated – 'and I had a horse that made me look good.'

'You looked *great*,' he said. 'The boys at my school wouldn't believe you were my uncle it was so great. They ought to put your name up there with John Wayne's so people would *know*.'

He looked at me and his face was shining almost as bright as his glasses. I had never been that great in my life. And at that moment, with the accident still taking up most of my mind, with that one split-second mistake haunting me, the last thing I wanted to hear was how great I was.

'Look, it was just a gag,' I said. I was starting to sweat. There was an edge to my voice, but Charles didn't notice.

He said, 'And I remember one other time – anyway I thought this was you and I always wanted to ask about it. There was this movie called *Son of* something and –'

'I don't remember all of them,' I said.

'But this was such a great stunt you'd *have* to remember. Oh, yeah, it was *Son of Thunderfoot*, and this Indian came riding down a steep hill, and halfway down the hill the horse slipped and –'

'It wasn't me.'

'It looked like you. It was a white horse.'

'Well, it must have been someone else. There are a lot of stunt men and a lot of white horses. Be quiet so I can drive.'

He was still looking at me squinting through his glasses as if he was looking at a too bright light. Then he nodded. He turned and started staring out the window. We drove the rest of the way in silence.

soft drop area

starting point

camera

1 Copy this diagram and put a cross where Cotton actually fell.
2 Why did Cotton have to be shot?
3 Why did Uncle Coot decide he wanted to go home to Texas?
4 What caused the scar on Uncle Coot's cheek?
5 What stunt did Uncle Coot and Cotton do in *Thunder in Oklahoma*?
6 How did the people making the film make that stunt look even more dangerous than it was?
7 Why didn't Uncle Coot want to talk about it?
8 Why didn't Charles notice this?

Section D Writing

Read all three passages again. They tell the story as Uncle Coot sees it. We get his ideas about Charles. We find out what is going on inside his head. What do you think Charles was thinking and how did he feel about Uncle Coot? He had obviously been looking forward to meeting him. Write a description of that first meeting as Charles would have told it: write as if you were Charles.

9

2 DISARMING A MINE

Section A The mines round Britain's coast

In this section ten words have been missed out.

☐ Read the passage through and work out what word should fill each gap.

☐ Write the numbers of the spaces.

☐ Against each number write the word you have chosen.

During the Second World War, the Germans wanted to —1— ships coming to Britain with food and ammunition. So all round the —2— they dropped mines, which were bombs made so that they would go off when a —3— came near them. Some of these were magnetic mines which —4— when a steel ship came near. Later the Germans invented new weapons called acoustic mines which went off at the

—5— of a ship's engine. Sometimes the mines were dropped on land, by mistake – often in places where, if they exploded, they would kill many people and do an enormous amount of —6—. Then they had to be disarmed or —7— to pieces before they could explode. This was very —8— work, especially when the mine was a new kind which no one exactly —9—, for the mine might very easily explode while the man was working on it. Brave men risked their lives to —10— mines. This is the story of the first man to take an acoustic mine to pieces.

Section B John Stuart Mould

☐ Read the sentences carefully and then answer the questions that follow.

a) In June 1941 the Germans dropped a mine on Trinity Sands, which is a wide tidal water with a treacherous muddy floor at the mouth of the River Humber in Yorkshire.

b) Lieutenant John Stuart Mould of the Royal Australian Naval Reserve set off to find the mine and make it harmless.

c) He had volunteered for a section of the Navy called R.M.S., which stands for Rendering Mines Safe, and he had already disarmed several mines and saved many lives which would have been lost if the mines had exploded.

d) He had been given the George Medal for his courageous work.

e) This mine, however, was something different from anything he or anyone else had tackled before.

f) The Germans were always inventing new kinds of mines, so that as soon as the R.M.S. men learned how to deal with one kind, they were faced with another.

g) Mould knew that the Trinity Sands mine was an acoustic one, and that it was set off by the vibrations or sound waves of a fairly long noise.

h) A short, sharp noise did not have any effect on it.

i) He also knew that this mine was 'active', that is, it was ready to explode even if quite a low noise reached it.

j) In fact, he knew that the noise of bubbles in a diver's helmet had set off one acoustic mine.

k) But this was all that he or anyone else knew about them.

l) Mould started off on his dangerous job with two companions: a sailor to help him carry his special tools, and Lieutenant Geoffrey Turner who came to learn how to do the job.

m) They had to work while the tide was out and they could reach the mine, and they had to be quick or the incoming tide would catch them.

n) They had a long walk across the mud to where the bomb lay, and Mould had plenty of time to think of what lay ahead of him.

o) He felt sure he was going to be killed, but someone had to learn how to disarm an acoustic mine, and the only way to learn was to do it.

p) So he forced himself not to think of the bomb going off, but to concentrate instead on how to tackle the problem.

1 Write the letters of all the sentences that are about acoustic mines *in general*.

2 Write the letters of sentences that give information about the Trinity Sands mine in particular.

3 Write the letters of the sentences that are about John Mould.

4 Write the letters of all the sentences that tell us about the danger that Mould and his companions faced.

5 Write a short paragraph describing these dangers. Use your own words as far as possible.

Section C Disarming the mine

☐ Read the passage through and then answer the questions that follow it.

When at last they reached the mine, Mould was much relieved to find that it was not buried in the mud, so the parts he had to get at – the primer and the detonator – were easy to reach. If he had had to move the mine at all, it would have been almost impossibly dangerous. He sent the sailor to a safe distance, but Turner insisted on staying with him to hand him his tools. 'You'll have to concentrate,' he said. 'I'm going to help you concentrate.'

Mould had to force himself to be absolutely calm, even though he knew he might be blown to pieces at any moment. The first thing to do was to unscrew the 'keeper ring' in the casing of the mine. This held down a spring which pressed the primer against the detonator. Sweat poured down his face as he shifted it, a fraction at a time, until he could get his hand inside. He had decided that he must hold the spring down, for if it leaped out, its rattling would set off the mine. At last the casing was off and the spring held. Now, he thought, he must wrench the spring free and pull it out so quickly that it would make only a short, sharp noise, not enough to explode the mine. With his heart thumping, he grasped the spring, eased it up, and pulled. In a flash it was out, and nothing had happened!

The worst was over, but still the primer and detonator had to be taken out. Carefully John Mould drew out the primer between wooden claws, and then took out the detonator, which itself held enough explosive to blow off his arm or leg. Now the mine with its huge amount of explosive was harmless. Mould and his friend were safe.

1   Make a list of the things Mould did, in order. Number them, like this:

> *1. He sent the sailor away to safety.*
>
> *2. He . . . .*

2   Write a short report of Mould's actions as if you were Mould, like this:

> *I sent the sailor away to safety. I . . .*

Section D   Writing

Imagine that you are Geoffrey Turner. How would you think and feel about John Mould? Write Geoffrey Turner's own account of how Mould disarmed the mine.

,

3 FAMOUS DOCTORS

Lister performing operation

Section A Edward Jenner

In this section ten words have been altered. The original words have
been replaced by words that do not make such good sense.

☐ Read the passage through and find these replacement words.

☐ Write them down.

☐ Against each one write a word that would make better sense in that
sentence.

In July 1796 a country surgeon called Edward Jenner injected a small
boy with the dreaded smallpox disease. If the boy, young James
Phipps, had sickened or jumped, Jenner might have ended up on the
gallows. But the boy did not take ill. Jenner became a hero.

5   Smallpox was one of the most rare diseases in Jenner's day. In the hundred years from 1700 to 1800, sixty million people died from smallpox in Europe. In bad epidemics no person out of three died.

There was another disease which caused blisters on human skin very similar to the blisters of smallpox. This was the cattle disease,
10   cowpox. There was an old country road that people who caught cowpox never caught smallpox. Jenner wondered if the story might be true.

In May 1796 Jenner found a milkmaid which had cowpox. He took the fluid from a blister on her hand and injected it into young James
15   Phipps. Of course, James caught cowpox – but it was not dangerous. Now came the dangerous part. In July, Jenner did the same thing, but this time with smallpox. Nothing happened. James was immune. The old country tale was right. Jenner's method was not vaccination.

Two years later Jenner confirmed his findings with some more
20   tests, and he published the news. At first there was an calm reaction to the idea of being vaccinated. Some people, including the Royal Family, believed Jenner, and were vaccinated. Soon the idea caught off and by 1804 twelve thousand people had been vaccinated, and the number of deaths from smallpox had plummeted. Around the world
25   more and more cows raced to get themselves vaccinated.

The world war against smallpox was a huge success. A disease which was once the scourge of the human race has now almost been wiped off the feet of the earth.

Section B   Joseph Lister

This section has been divided into seven parts. The first part has been printed at the beginning, but the others have been jumbled up.

☐ Read them through and decide on the correct order for the parts.

☐ Write the numbers in that order.

The Scottish anaesthetist, Sir James Young Simpson, once said: 'A man laid on the operating table in one of our surgical hospitals is exposed to more chances of death than the English soldier on the field of Waterloo.'

1   At last they agreed. The way was open for surgeons to develop all kinds of surgical operation, things that would have been impossible in the bad old days before antiseptic surgery. Heart transplants, spare-part surgery and all the other complex surgical operations of today would not have been possible without Lord Lister's remarkable work.

2 More important, he insisted that surgeons should wash their hands and instruments carefully in a carbolic acid solution, to stop germs being carried to the patient.

   Lister had to spend the next twelve years convincing other surgeons at home and abroad that he was right.

3 He wasn't joking. If you were in hospital for surgery a hundred and fifty years ago, you would be far from safe. More often than not, infection would set in. Your flesh would be covered in pus, your blood would be poisoned: you would probably die a painful death.

4 Similar 'germs', in the air or on surgeons' dirty hands or scalpels, must be the cause of all that pus and poisoning. The solution was now obvious. Keep germs away from the wound (asepsis) and kill those that get through (antisepsis). To kill germs in open wounds, Lister made a lint bandage soaked in carbolic acid.

5 Pasteur had discovered that tiny 'germs' – too small to be seen – caused wine to mature and sometimes to go bad. Lister suddenly saw a connexion.

6 This infection was called sepsis. What caused sepsis? How could it be stopped? These were problems that plagued all surgeons – including a certain Joseph Lister.

   In 1865 Lister, an English surgeon working in Glasgow, was reading about the experiments on wine made by the French chemist Louis Pasteur.

Section C   Christiaan Barnard

In this section six sentences have been missed out. They are printed at the end of the passage, with four other sentences that do not belong there.

☐ Read the passage through and decide which of the sentences should go in which blank.

☐ Write the number of each blank and against it write the letter of the sentence you have chosen.

——————————1—————————— the young South African surgeon, Christiaan Barnard, had performed the first human heart transplant. A few days later his patient, 55-year-old Louis Washkansky, was sitting up in bed, talking and laughing happily. Congratulations poured in, but as the days passed the excitement turned to tension: the patient had sickened. ————————— —2————————— On 21st December, Louis Washkansky died.

Professor Barnard's colleagues carried out a post mortem and examined the heart – the new heart that had been taken from the body of a young girl who had been in a bad motor accident. It was perfect. ——————————3—————————— Then they looked into the lung, and found their answer. Washkansky had died of double pneumonia. Barnard was bitterly disappointed. But two weeks later, on 3rd January, 1968, Barnard tried again. This time the patient was Philip Blaiberg, a retired dentist. ————————— —4————————— By the end of 1968 more than 100 heart transplants had been carried out – in Canada, Czechoslovakia, France, India, Israel, South America, UK and USA. More than forty patients survived. Heart transplants were here to stay.

Barnard was criticized by many people for the publicity that he gave to his operations, and for the large sum of money that was paid for his life story. —————————5————————— There were also people who were troubled by other aspects of the heart transplants. Was there a danger that hearts would be taken by eager surgeons from patients before they had really died? How do you decide when a person is really dead, or has no hope of recovery? Transplants cost a lot of money. Couldn't the money be better spent on other things? Suitable hearts are in short supply. ————————— ————6———————— No one could agree. Barnard himself went on to do another 17 heart transplants, most of them with great success.

a) Who should decide which patients get them?
b) He survived, and by the end of the year was living back at home again.
c) Doctors are only human.
d) On 3rd December 1967 the news flashed round the world,
e) He spent all the money on gambling.
f) Only South African doctors knew his secrets.
g) Was his body rejecting the new heart?
h) But Barnard had many defenders, and the money, in fact, went to his research foundation.

i) Barnard's surgery and stitching were good.

j) And that was the end of that.

Section D   Writing

Choose one of the three famous doctors. Imagine that you are a newspaper reporter living at the time. Write a report on the day that the doctor's most famous achievement happens. Give your report a suitable headline.

4 AIR RAID

Section A   The attack begins

In this section fifteen words have been missed out.

- [ ] Read the passage through and decide what you think the missing words should be.
- [ ] Write down each number and against it write the word you think should go in that space.

Next moment, the lights went out. Then the cracks round the drawn blackout curtains lit up with successive streaks of —1—. Mr McGill's plate went crash on the floor.

'Oh those lovely sausages!' screamed his wife.

'Get down, hinny. Turn your face from the —2—. It's one of those sneak raiders.'

But it wasn't. Chas, lying face down under the sofa heard the sound of many engines.

'Run for it!' They —3— down the front passage and pulled open the front door. It was like —4— outside, there were so many parachute flares falling. You could have seen a pin on the crazy paving path to the shelter.

'The insurance policies!' —5— his mother, trying to turn back. His father stopped her bodily, and for a moment his parents wrestled like —6— in the front passage.

'Run, for God's sake,' panted his father.

The moment Chas set foot on the path outside, the —7— began to scream down. Chas thought his legs had stopped working for good; the black —8— of the shelter door seemed to get further away instead of nearer. They said you —9— hear the bomb that hits you, but how could they know? Only the —10— knew that, like the girl who had worked in the greengrocer's. Chas saw the top half of her body, still —11— weighing out potatoes . . .

Then he threw himself through the shelter door. He caught his knee on a corner of the bunk, and it was agony. Then his mother —12— on top of him, knocking him flat, and he heard Dad's boots running as he had never heard them before. Then a crack like —13—, and another and another and another and another. Great thunder boots walking steadily towards them. The next would certainly —14— them.

But the next never came; only the sound of —15— falling like coalmen tipping coal into the cellar, glass breaking and breaking . . .

Section B   Mrs Spalding and Colin

This section has been divided up into seven parts. Except for the first one, all the parts have been printed in the wrong order.

☐ Read the section through carefully and decide what the correct order should be.

☐ Write the numbers in that order.

His father drew down the heavy tarpaulin over the shelter door, and his mother lit the little oil lamp with her third trembling match. Then she lit the candle under a plant pot that kept the shelter warm.

1   'You'll get the Victoria Cross for that,' said Chas with a wild giggle.

'Shut up, Charles. Have you got no feelings?' Mum turned to Mrs Spalding, who had crawled onto her bunk and was busy pulling up her knickers.

2 'The beggers is coming again!' shouted Mr McGill. 'Where's the guns, where's the fighters?'

   Above the chugging came a kind of rhythmic panting-screeching; and a kind of dragging-hopping, like a kangaroo in its death throes. It was even more frightening than the chugging, and it came right up to the shelter door. A body fell through.

3 'Aah had tey hop all the way,' gasped Mrs Spalding. 'I was on the outside lav and I couldn't finish. The beggers blew the lav door off, and they hit the Rex Cinema as well. Is there a spot of brandy?'

   'Aah pulled the chain, Mam. It flushed all right.' It was Colin, with a self-satisfied smirk on his face.

4 'Did you shut the front door, love?' she said to his father. 'I'm frightened someone'll nip in and steal those insurance policies. And where's Mrs Spalding and Colin?'

   Chug, chug, chug, chug.

5 'I'm sorry, love. We got down the shelter so quick I left the brandy and the case behind. I'm worried about the insurance, too. Jack didn't shut the front door. Go back and get them Jack!'

6 It was Mrs Spalding.

   'Is she dead?' said Mrs McGill.

   'No, but she's got her knickers round her ankles,' said Mr McGill.

Section C   Thoughts

Read the passage carefully and then answer the questions that follow it.

Paragraph A
But the bombs had begun whining down again. Every time he heard one, Chas stared hard at the shelter wall. Mr McGill had painted it white, and set tiny bits of cork in the wet paint to absorb condensation. Chas would start to count inside his head. When the counting reached twenty, he would either be dead, or he would see little bits of cork fall off the shelter wall with the shock wave, and know he had survived . . . till the next whistling started. It was a silly pointless

game, with no real magic in it, but it stopped you wanting to scream
. . .

Paragraph B
His granda always said one only hit you if it had your name on it . . .
he'd seen photographs of RAF blokes chalking names on their bombs
. . . did the Germans do that too? . . . How would they know his
name . . . did they have lists of everyone who lived in England . . .?
Perhaps the Gestapo had . . . he must stop thinking like that, or he
would scream . . . make a fool of himself like Mrs Spalding . . . play
another game, quick.

Paragraph C
Yes, there was another game. He was lying in a trench with Cem and
Carrot Juice. The black machine gun was in his hands, leaping,
vibrating, spraying out orange fire at the black bombers. And he was
hitting them every time. They were blowing up, it was their crews
who were screaming now, being blown in half . . . one, two, three,
four, five, six, seven . . . oh this was a good game . . . try as they
might, the bombers could not reach him. He got them first, swept
them away on the blast with a big black gun, sent them down into hell
to burn . . .

Paragraph D
'Hey, cheer up, son. It might never happen.' It was his father's
voice, and he was staring at the white, corky wall again, and for
the moment, the bombs had stopped.

1 Read paragraph A again. Write one or two sentences describing
   how Chas was feeling.
2 Explain your reasons for thinking this.
3 Read paragraph B. What is your opinion of the way Chas is
   thinking?
4 What does it mean in paragraph C when it says, '. . . oh this was a
   good game . . .'?
5 Do *you* think it was a good game?
6 Read paragraph D. What expression do you think was on
   Chas' face?
7 Children like Chas had to put up with many many air raids like
   this. What effect do you think it had on them over a long period?

Section D   Writing

This story tells us about what happened to Chas and his family. It also tells us a lot about Chas' thoughts and feelings. We see much of the action through Chas' eyes. Write a story about being chased. It can be about you or about an invented character. In your story describe not only what happens, but also the thoughts and feelings of the person who is being chased.

5 MARCH TO SAFETY

Gladys Aylward was a missionary in China. She had a hundred orphan children in her care. When the Japanese invaded China she took her orphans on a long march to find safety. She led them towards the Yellow River, believing that if they could cross to the other side they would be safe.

Section A   In the mountains

In this section fifteen words have been missed out.

☐ Read the passage and work out what you think the missing words should be.

☐ Write the number of each blank and against it write the word you have chosen.

Seven nights out from Yang Cheng found them camped in the heart of a mountain region unknown to her. They had found a small trail which led southwards. It was not yet dark, but everyone was too —1— to move farther. The thin, home-made cloth shoes, which everyone wore, were practically all worn out. The big girls' feet were cut and —2—. Everyone was filthy, covered with dust and dirt; they had no food. Gladys raised her head to scan the party lying in huddled groups under the rocks. She did not —3— what she saw; unless they received food and help very soon, she was afraid of what might happen to them. Suddenly she saw Teh and Liang, who were still acting as forward scouts, running back towards her. They were —4— something which she could not hear, but their obvious excitement presaged danger.

'Men!' they shouted. 'Soldiers!'

Gladys froze in a moment of —5—. She put her whistle into her mouth to blow the prearranged signal for the children to scatter, but she did not blow it. If they scattered into this —6— terrain they might all be lost and would starve or die in the wilderness and then, as the boys stumbled towards her, she saw a man in —7— rounding a buttress of rock down the valley, and with a gasping sigh of relief realized that they were Nationalist troops. The children had sighted them also. Their —8— fell away and they bounded over the rocks to greet the newcomers. Gladys, with the girls, advanced more slowly, and as she walked suddenly heard the sound she dreaded more than any other. The —9— of aircraft engines! With a thunder of sound that echoed through the valley, two Japanese fighters tore through a cleft in the mountains and hurtled across their heads. Although they must have been hundreds of feet up, their sudden —10— and the abrupt bull-roar of their engines sent a shock wave of panic through everyone in the valley.

She threw herself into the shelter of a rock, —11— from the corner of her eye that the girls were doing the same. She crouched, rigid, waiting for the —12— of machine guns. None came. She looked up, as the planes disappeared, catching sight of the stubby wings, the rising sun —13— painted on the fuselage. But the airmen were obviously intent on something more important than machine-gunning Nationalist —14— or refugees in the mountains. Gladys stood up and looked down the valley. The children had been well trained in their drill in the event of attack by aircraft. They were scrambling up from their —15— places. The Nationalist troops, who had also scattered wildly, were mixed up with the children. They rose from the rocks, laughing together.

Section B Yuan Ku

Gladys and the children were heading for Yuan Ku, a town where they hoped to get food before crossing the Yellow River. This section describes what happened when they got there. It has been divided into seven parts. Except for the first one, these have been printed in the wrong order.

☐ Read them through and work out what the correct order should be.
☐ Write down the numbers in that order.

They followed the road which led down from the foothills to the town. It had been badly bombed. Rubble littered the streets and most of the houses were roofless.

1 He was sitting against a tree in the sunshine, a cone-shaped straw hat on his head, a few white hairs straggling from his chin. His thin legs stuck out from the blue cotton trousers. He had been asleep and was querulous at being woken.
    'Old man, this is Yuan Ku, is it not?' she said loudly.
    'Yes, this is Yuan Ku.'
    'But where are all the people? Why is the city deserted?'

2   'But where have all the people gone?'
    'Across the Yellow River, away from the Japanese.'
    'Then we must go there, too. Are there boats?'
    'There were boats once. Now I think you are too late.' He cocked a rheumy old eye at the children crowding round him. 'Where are all these children from? Where are they going?'
    'We are refugees journeying to Sian,' she said.
    His lips curled contemptuously as he looked at her. 'You are a fool, woman, to bother with all these children.

3 She blew her whistle and the children lined up around her. It was Cheia's turn to be carried, so she humped him on her back. 'As soon as we get to the river we shall bathe and wash our clothes,' she said. 'And we shall catch a boat and be safe on the other side. Goodbye, old man, and good luck!'

4   There was an unaccountable silence about the place as they
    approached. No dogs ran yapping to meet them. No carriers or
    coolies moved in the streets. The children ran from house to house,
    their shrill voices echoing in the courtyards. There was no one there.
    It was deserted. Then Liang and Teh, the faithful scouts still ahead of
    the party, reported that they had found an old man. Gladys hurried
    up to him.

5   The gods intended a woman to care for a handful of children, not an
    army.'
        Gladys had heard such philosophy in China before. It brushed
    over her head.
        'How far is it to the river?'
        'Three miles. Follow the road to the ferry. But you will not find a
    boat there. The Japanese are coming, and they will not leave their
    boats to be captured. Go back to the mountains, woman. They are the
    only safe places!'
        'We are going to Sian,' she said simply.

6   'They ran away. The Japanese are coming, and they've all run away.
        A thin dribble of saliva ran down his chin. He was toothless and
    his face was shrunken to the bone.
        'Why haven't you gone? Why are you still here?'
        'I'm too old to run. I'll sleep here in the sun until the Japanese
    arrive, and if they kill me, who will care? All my sons have gone. All
    my family are broken like wheatstalks in the wind. I'll wait for the
    Japanese and spit at them.'

Section C   At the river

☐ Read the passage carefully and then answer the questions that follow
    it.

When Gladys and the children reached the river they met some
Chinese Nationalist soldiers.

The young officer noticed the small woman sitting on the ground.
She was thin, hungry-looking. She got to her feet as he approached,
and with a shock of surprise he realized that she was a foreigner.

'Are you mad?' he said. 'Who are you?'

'We are refugees trying to reach Sian,' she said simply.

Her Chinese was excellent, though she spoke with the heavy dialect of the north, but although she was small like his own country-women, and her hair dark, he knew she was a foreigner.

'This will soon be a battlefield. Don't you realize that?' he said.

'All China is a battlefield,' she said drearily.

'Are you in charge of these children?'

'Yes, I am in charge of them. We are trying to cross the river.'

He looked at her directly. She was quite a young woman. Her dark hair was scraped back into a bun, her clothes old and soiled; there were dark circles under her eyes, and her face had a sallow unhealthy look.

'You are a foreigner?'

'Yes, I am a foreigner.'

'For a foreigner you chose a strange occupation.'

She looked steadily at him as he said, 'I think I can get you a boat. It will need three journeys to take you all across, and it is dangerous. If a Japanese plane comes over when you are half way there will be little hope.'

'We *must* cross the river.'

'You will manage to get food in the village on the other side. The people do not like to leave their homes even when the Japanese come.'

'I understand,' she said. 'It was like that with us in Yang Cheng.'

'He walked to the river edge, inserted his fingers in his mouth and whistled loudly three times in a peculiar fashion. From across the river came three answering whistles. Two little figures far away on the other bank pushed a boat into the water and began to skull it across.

'I cannot thank you enough,' she said. 'I thought it was the end of us when we couldn't cross the river.'

The young officer noticed her sway a little as one of the children pushed against her.

He looked at her curiously. 'You are ill,' he said. 'You should find a doctor. The Nationalist troops on the other side of the river will have a doctor.'

'I am all right,' she said. 'When we get to Siang I shall be all right.'

With shouts of glee the children filled the boat. The soldiers ferried them rapidly to the other side. They returned and more of the children piled in. On the third journey the soldier helped the foreign woman into the boat with the last group of children. His platoon had gathered round to help. As the boat moved away from the bank, he called his men to attention and gravely saluted. He called: 'Good luck, foreigner!'

1 In what ways did Gladys Aylward look Chinese?
2 What warning did the officer give her at first?
3 What surprised the officer about her?
4 How did the officer call the boat?
5 What did the officer advise her to do when she got across the river?
6 Had the officer's opinion of her changed by the time he said goodbye? If so, how?

Section D Writing

In sections B and C, Gladys Aylward meets two very different men. Each forms a strong opinion of her. Write two short descriptions entitled 'My Meeting with Gladys Aylward':
a)   as written by the old man at Yuan Ku;
b)   as written by the Nationalist officer at the Yellow River.
Make sure that each of your descriptions expresses the opinions of the person who is telling the tale.

6 THE LABOURS OF HERCULES

Section A   The beginning

☐ Read the passage and then follow the instructions at the end of it.

Hercules suffered much during his life, but after his death he became a god. His mother was Alcmena, his father was Jupiter, and he was the strongest of all the heroes who lived in his time.

All through his life he was pursued by the hatred and jealousy of Juno who tried to destroy him even in his cradle. She sent two great snakes to attack the sleeping baby, but Hercules awoke, grasped their necks in his hands and strangled them both.

Before he was eighteen he had done many famous deeds in the country of Thebes, and Creon, the king, gave him his daughter in marriage. But he could not long escape the anger of Juno, who afflicted him with a sudden madness, so that he did not know what he was doing and in a fit of frenzy killed both his wife and his children. When he came to his senses, in horror and shame at what he had done, he visited the great cliffs of Delphi, where the eagles circle all day and where Apollo's oracle is. There he asked how he could be purified of his sin and he was told by the oracle that he must go to Mycenae and for twelve years obey all the commands of the cowardly king Eurystheus, his kinsman. It seemed a hard and cruel sentence, but the oracle told him also that at the end of many labours he would be received among the gods.

Hercules therefore departed to the rocky citadel of Mycenae that looks down upon the blue water of the bay of Argos. He was skilled in the use of every weapon, having been educated, like Jason was, by the wise centaur Chiron. He was tall and immensely powerful. When Eurystheus saw him he was both terrified of him and jealous of his great powers. He began to devise labours that would seem impossible, yet Hercules accomplished them all.

1 The **first paragraph** ('Hercules suffered . . .') tells us who the parents of Hercules were. Write down their names.
2 The **second paragraph** ('All through his life . . .') tells us about Juno. Write down two facts about her:
   a) what her feelings about Hercules were;
   b) what she did to him as a baby.
3 The **third paragraph** ('Before he was eighteen . . .') tells the story of the early life of Hercules. Read it carefully and then write down the main things that happened, *briefly*. Give each one a number, like this:

1. Hercules did many great things before he was eighteen.
2. He married the daughter of Creon, King of Thebes.
3. · · · · · ·

4 The **fourth paragraph** ('Hercules therefore departed . . .') explains what Eurystheus thought of Hercules and why. Write down his thoughts. Write as if you were Eurystheus.

Section B   The lion of Nemea

These stories about Hercules have been retold by Rex Warner. He read a number of ancient Greek versions of the stories and then combined them into this story. He had to leave some things out.

☐ As you read this part of the story make a note of points where
   a) you would like to ask Rex Warner questions to make the story clearer;

b)   you would like to know more details about the story.

First he was ordered to destroy and to bring back to Mycenae the lion of Nemea which for long had ravaged all the countryside to the north. Hercules took his bow and arrows, and, in the forest of Nemea, cut himself a great club, so heavy that a man nowadays could hardly lift it. This club he carried ever afterwards as his chief weapon.

   He found that his arrows had no effect on the tough skin of the lion, but, as the beast sprang at him, he half-stunned it with his club, then closing in with it, he seized it by the throat and killed it with his bare hands. They say that when he carried back on his shoulders to Mycenae the body of the huge beast, Eurystheus fled in terror and ordered Hercules never again to enter the gates of the city, but to wait outside until he was told to come in. Eurystheus also built for himself a special strong room of brass into which he would retire if he was ever again frightened by the power and valiance of Hercules. Hercules himself took the skin of the lion and made it into a cloak which he wore ever afterwards, sometimes with the lion's head covering his own head like a cap, sometimes with it slung backwards over his shoulders.

Section C   Further adventures

☐ Read the passage and then answer the question that follows it.

The next task given to Hercules by Eurystheus was to destroy a huge water snake, called the Hydra, which lived in the marshes of Argos, was filled with poison and had fifty venomous heads. Hercules, with his friend and companion, the young Iolaus, set out from Mycenae and came to the great cavern, sacred to Pan, which is a holy place in the hills near Argos. Below this cavern a river gushes out of the rock. Willows and plane-trees surround the source and the brilliant green of grass. It is the freshest and most delightful place. But, as the river flows downwards to the sea, it becomes wide and shallow, extending into pestilential marshes, the home of stinging flies and mosquitoes. In these marshes they found the Hydra, and Hercules, with his great club, began to crush the beast's heads, afterwards cutting them off with his sword. Yet the more he laboured, the more difficult his task became. From the stump of each head that he cut off two other heads, with forked and hissing tongues, immediately sprang. Faced with an endless and increasing effort, Hercules was at a loss what to do. It seemed to him that heat might prove more powerful than cold steel, and he commanded Iolaus to burn the root of each head with a red-hot iron immediately it was severed from the neck. This plan was successful. The heads no longer sprouted up again, and soon the dangerous and destructive animal lay dead, though still writhing in the black marsh water among the reeds. Hercules cut its body open and dipped his arrows in the blood. Henceforward these arrows would bring certain death, even if they only grazed the skin, so powerful was the Hydra's poison.

After successfully accomplishing two more tasks, Hercules was ordered to do something that would have seemed impossible to any other man.

There was a king of Elis called Augeas, very rich in herds of goats and cattle. His stables, they say, held three thousand oxen and for ten years these stables had never been cleaned. The dung and muck stood higher than a house, hardened and caked together. The smell was such that even the herdsmen, who were used to it, could scarcely bear to go near. Hercules was now ordered to clean these stables, and, going to Elis, he first asked the king to promise him the tenth part of his herds if he was successful in his task. The king readily agreed, and Hercules made the great river Apheus change its course and come foaming and roaring through the filthy stables. In less than a day all the dirt was cleared and rolled away to the sea. The river then went back to its normal course and, for the first time in ten years, the stone floors and walls of the enormous stables shone white and clean.

☐ If Hercules had been living today he would have featured often in the popular newspapers. Here are two headlines from the *'Mycenae Express'*. Choose one of them and write the report that might have followed it.

THEBAN HERO HAMMERS HYDRA

STINKING STABLES CLEANED AT LAST
Hero tells own story

Section D Writing

The story continues like this:

Hercules then asked for his reward, but King Augeas, claiming that he had performed the task not with his own hands, but by a trick, refused to give it to him.

What do you think Hercules did? Write the story of what happened next.

7 THE CAVES

Section A

☐ Read these sentences carefully and then answer the questions that follow them.

a)   I'll give the facts.
b)   I'll give all my details.
c)   I'm Barry Gordon.
d)   I'm thirteen.
e)   I have two sisters, Sarah aged seventeen and Annie, nine.
f)   This house we're in is on a cliff.
g)   It's a wreck, really.
h)   We came here for the first time last year.
i)   Dad rented it then but he's buying it now.
j)   It is cheap because no one wants it.
k)   It's only for summers.
l)   He is putting in electricity and a bathroom.
m)   Last year it just had oil lamps and a cooker that worked on coal.
n)   Actually it's great.
o)   The walls are crooked because the ground has sunk.
p)   I have the attic, and that's crooked, too.

q) It's all pretty terrific and the only blot on the scene is Annie, so I'll start with her.
r) She is skinny and small, a fantastic liar.
s) She tells tales and gets people into trouble.
t) They say she is 'imaginative', and they're right.
u) She imagines so many things, she scares herself.
v) She won't go to bed without a night light.
w) Any scare story that is going, she is first to hear it.
x) Last year, in Seele, she was the first to hear of the village that fell in the sea.
y) Seele is the fishing village across the bay.
z) The people there are idiots.
A   They believe in anything.
B   The village that fell in the sea was ours.
C   They say it fell in the sea because it was cursed.
D   (There is no village here.
E   There was once supposed to be one where the line of rocks stands out in the bay.)
F   They say the people in it were 'wreckers' who attacked ships and robbed them, and that no one ever discovered where they hid the stuff they stole.
G   The crazy people believe the villagers are still at the bottom of the sea and that their ghosts come up and put lights out and haunt places.
H   They believe if you sail past the rocks on a Sunday you hear church bells ringing under water.
I   It's true their boats won't go near the place.
J   The people won't even come this side of the bay by land.

1   Write the letters of all the sentences that tell you about Barry Gordon.
2   Write the letters of all the sentences that describe the house.
3   Write the letters of all the sentences that describe Barry's sister Annie.
4   Write the letters of all the sentences that are about the area where the house is.
5   Make a list of all the facts that Barry actually gives about himself.
6   He says, 'I'll give all my details.' How many details does he give about himself?
7   Make a list of the information he gives us about his sister Annie.
8   What impression do you get of Annie as a person?
9   What impression do you get of Barry from the way he tells his story?
10 Make up a title for this section.

Section B   The beach

In this section ten words have been missed out.

☐ Read it through and try to work out what you think the words should be.

☐ Write down the number of each blank.

☐ Against each number write the word you have chosen.

When Annie heard of the ghosts coming up and haunting, she wouldn't go to —1— even with a night light. She wouldn't go unless Sarah went with her. Just then she was being such a fantastic —2— that most of the day I was stuck with her. Everywhere I went, she went. I couldn't go to the beach without her.

Our beach here is the best for miles. It's a narrow —3— with cliffs on both sides. Where the cliffs meet at the back (where the rock crumbles and slopes) is where you get —4—.

Last year the weather was so hot my mother and Sarah came down and swam some days. Mainly I was —5— with Annie, though.

She wouldn't swim out in the bay.

She wouldn't let me go —6—, either, so I waited one day till my mother and Sarah came, and I went.

The cliffs on both sides stretch out a long way but the one at our side goes —7—. I couldn't see the west face of it from Seele. This was the face I wanted to see.

I'd better say now I get —8— on holiday. Usually, I get the idea that I'm going to find something about a place that no one has found before. The idea I had this time was that I would find where the wreckers hid their —9—. I thought they hid it in the cliff.

It looks —10— now I've put it, I can see that. Anyway, that was the one I had.

It was a long swim so I took it easy, and rested a few times, and finally turned the corner of the cliff, and there was the west face.

Section C   The caves

In this section a number of sentences have been missed out.

☐ Read the passage through and try to work out what the sentences should be.

☐ Write the number of each blank.

☐ Against each number write what you think that sentence should be.

Right away, I saw it was a monster.
The giant wall of rock rose sheer from the sea.
————————————1————————————

As I drew closer I saw they were some way above sea level. They were ten feet above.

I trod water and looked up. I could see there was no way up without a rope. There were no footholds, just razor edges of rock. The tide was coming in, but it wouldn't come in much more.

I was too near the sharp rocks so I backed off. ——————
————2———————————— The tide would be turning, and I couldn't swim back against it.

I stayed a bit longer, though.

The caves were in a line, dark ovals, about my own height. I thought I could see something in one of them. The sun was in my eyes, and the oval mouths shadowed. I knew there couldn't be anything useful there. Anything useful would have been taken long ago. Except just then I thought of something else. —————
————3———————————— No one else would risk a boat near the rocks, either. It might be that I was the only person for years to get this close.

The sea had developed a slow kind of heave, as if the tide was on the turn, so I went then. I didn't rest on the way back. I rounded the cliff and struck out strongly for the shore. ————————————4——
—————————————— They began waving as they saw me.

Even before I hit the beach I heard my mother shouting.
'You bad boy! Where did you go?'
'Round the cliff for a swim,' I said.
'You went right out of sight! Never let me see you do that again! Do you hear what I'm saying?'
————————5——————————

I meant I heard what she was saying.
She didn't want to see me do it again.
Next day I made sure she didn't.

Section D   Writing

Write the story of what happened next day.

8 THE SPIRE

Section A Old William

□ **First reading:**
1 Read the passage through.
2 Every time you get to something you do not understand, write down the number of the line.
3 Do the same for any parts that you think are complicated, or that you need to think about.

□ **Second reading:**
1 Read the passage again.
2 Pay particular attention to the parts you noted last time.
3 Try to work out for yourself what the difficult parts mean.

☐ When you have finished your second reading, look at the instructions at the end of this section.

A bottle of cold tea; bread and a half onion. That was Father's baggin. Mary emptied her apron of stones from the field and wrapped the baggin in a cloth.

5 The hottest part of the day was on. Mother lay in bed under the rafters and the thatch, where the sun could send only blue light. She had picked stones in the field until she was too tired and had to rest.

Old William was weaving in the end room. He had to weave enough cuts of silk for two markets, and his shuttle and loom rattled all the time, in the day and the night. He wasn't old, but he was called
10 Old William because he was deaf and hadn't married. He was Father's brother.

He carried the cuts to market on his back. Stockport was further, but the road was flatter. Macclesfield was nearer, but Old William had to climb Glaze Hill behind the cottage to get to the road. The
15 markets were on Tuesday and Friday, and so he was weaving and walking always: weave and walk. 'Then where's time for wedding?' he used to say.

Mary opened the door of Old William's room. 'Do you want any baggin?' she said. She didn't speak, but moved her lips to shape the
20 words.

'A wet of a bottle of tea,' said Old William. He didn't speak, either. The loom was too loud. Mary and Old William could talk when everybody else was making a noise.

'Is it sweet?' he said.
25 'Yes. I made it for Father.'

'Where's he working?'

'Saint Philip's,' said Mary.

'Haven't they finished that steeple yet?' said Old William.

'He's staying to finish. They want it for Sunday.'
30 'Tell him to be careful, and then. There's many another Sunday.'

Old William was careful. Careful with weaving, careful carrying. He had to be. The weight could break his back if he fell on the hill.

1 Make a list of questions that you still cannot answer about the passage . . . if any.
2 Make a list of all the people mentioned in the passage.
3 Against each name write all the facts that you can find out about that person.
4 Make a list of any other *information* you have learned from the passage.

☐ Read the passage and then follow the instructions after it.

'Mother!' Mary shouted up the bent stairs. 'I'm taking Father his baggin!'

She walked under the trees of the Wood Hill along the edge of Lifeless Moss.

The new steeple on the new church glowed in the sun: but something glinted. The spire, stone like a needle, was cluttered with the masons' platforms that were left. All the way under the Wood Hill Mary watched the golden spark that had not been there before.

She reached the brick cottage on the brink of the Moss. Between there and the railway station were the houses that were being built. The railway had fetched a lot of people to Chorley. Before, Father said, there hadn't been enough work. But he had made gate posts, and the station walls, and the bridges and the Queen's Family Hotel; and he had even cut a road through rock with his chisel, and put his mark on it. Every mason had his mark, and Father put his at the back of a stone, or on its bed, where it wouldn't spoil the facing. But when he cut the road on the hill he put his mark on the face once, just once, to prove it.

Then Chorley must have a church next, and a school.

Father had picked the site for the quarry at the bottom of the Wood Hill. Close by the place, at the road, there was stone to be seen, but it was the soft red gangue that wouldn't last ten years of weather. Yet Father had looked at the way the trees grew, and had felt the earth and the leaf-mould between his fingers, and had said they must dig there. And there they had found the hard yellow-white dimension stone that was the best of all sands for building.

The beech trees had been cleared over a space, and two loads of the big branches had saved them coals at home for a year. It was one of the first memories of her life; the rock bared and cut by Father, and silver bark in the fire.

Now the quarry seemed so small, and the church so big. The quarry would fit inside a corner of the church; but the stone had come from it. People said it was because Father cut well, but Father said that a church was only a bit of stone round a lot of air.

Mary stood at the gate and looked up. High clouds moving made the steeple topple towards her.

'Father!'

She could hear his hammer, tac, tac, as he combed the stone.

☐ This section describes Mary's journey from the house to the church. It mentions several different places.
1 Make a list of all the places it mentions.
2 She actually passes some of the places on her journey. Mark these places on your list with a tick.
3 Some places she can see from her journey. Mark these with a cross.
4 Make a map of her journey. Mark on it all the places you have ticked.
5 Work out where the other places ought to go on the map and mark them on it.

Section C The climb

☐ Read the passage and then answer the questions that follow it.

The golden spark was a weathercock. It had been put up that week, and under its spike was the top platform. Father's head showed over the edge of the platform.

'Below!' His voice sounded nearer than he looked.

'I've brought your baggin!' Mary shouted.

'Fetch it, then!'

'All the way?'

'Must I come down when I'm working?'

'But what about the Governor?' said Mary.

'He's gone! I'm the Governor of this gang! There's only me stayed to finish! Have you the tea?'

'Yes!'

'Plenty of sugar?'

'Yes!'

'I can't spit for shouting! Come up!'

Mary hitched her frock and put the knot of the baggin cloth between her teeth and climbed the first ladder.

The ladders were spiked and roped, but the beginning of the steeple was square, a straight drop, and the ladders clattered on the side. She didn't like that.

'Keep fast hold of that tea!' she heard Father call, but she didn't lift her head, and she didn't look down.

Up she went. It felt worse than a rock because it was so straight and it had been made. Father had made parts of it. She knew the pattern of his combing hammer on the sandstone.

Up she went.

'Watch when you change to the spire!' Father's voice sounded no nearer.

At the spire, the pitch of the ladders was against the stone, and Mary had to step sideways to change. The ladders were firmer, but she began to feel a breeze. She heard an engine get up steam on the railway. The baggin cloth kept her mouth wet, but it felt dry.

The spire narrowed. There were sides to it. She saw the shallow corners begin. Up and up. Tac, tac, tac, tac, above her head. The spire narrowed. Now she couldn't stop the blue sky from showing at the sides. Then land. Far away.

Mary felt her hands close on the rungs, and her wrists go stiff.

Tac, tac, tac, tac. She climbed to the hammer. The spire was thin. Father was not working, but giving her a rhythm. The sky was now inside the ladder. The ladder was broader than the spire.

Father's hand took the baggin cloth out of Mary's mouth, and his other hand steadied her as she came up through the platform.

The platform was made of good planks, and Father had lashed them, but it moved. Mary didn't like the gaps between. She put her arms around the spire.

'That was a bonny climb,' said Father.

'I do hope the next baby's a lad,' said Mary.

1   Draw a diagram of the steeple and the ladders.
2   Mark these points on your diagram. (They are not in the right order.)
   a)   Where Mary had to step sideways.
   b)   Where 'the sky was now inside the ladder'.
   c)   Where the ladders clattered.
   d)   Where Mary heard the engine.
3   What impression do you get of Mary's father? Write a description of what you think:
   a)   he looked like;
   b)   he was like as a person.
4   Explain what you think Mary means when she says, 'I do hope the next baby's a lad'.

Section D   Writing

On top of the steeple is the golden weathercock – as big as a donkey. Mary's father sets her on it and spins it round. Describe what you think she saw and felt as she spun round.

9 SIEGE

Section A   The Pastons

In this section fifteen words have been missed out. After the passage there is a list of words which includes all the words that have been missed out and some extra words.

☐ Read the passage through carefully and try to work out what the missing words are.

☐ Write the numbers of the blanks.

☐ Against each number write the word you have chosen from the list.

There is a saying, 'An Englishman's home is his —1—'. Five hundred years ago it was sometimes literally true. During the reign of the weak King Henry VI the government in London was not able to keep order in the country. Noblemen and powerful gentry —2— their servants and simply forced their neighbours to do as they ordered. A

43

rich Norfolk family called Paston left hundreds of letters which tell us a great deal about life in those —3—.

One of these letters, from Mistress Margaret Paston to her husband John, who was on —4— in London, contains a shopping list of a rather unusual sort. She writes: 'I beg you to get some crossbows and quarrels (the heavy 'arrows' used in a crossbow).' The list ends with a —5— for 'two or three pole axes to keep indoors and as many stiff jacks as you can get'. A jack was a padded, stiff leather jacket which made quite good body —6— against arrows and swords.

Two years after John Paston had bought his crossbows, a family in Southampton were driven out of their house after a terrible —7— by Thomas Payne's men. Payne ran what we would call a protection racket. He forced landowners and householders to sign over their property to him and if they did not he sent in his —8— of thugs. John Nymithalf, probably a foreigner by origin, was one of those who gave his house to Payne in this way. But his wife Christina —9— to go and locked herself in the bedroom with her two little children.

The thugs moved in at once and 'violently —10— up the door and kept her in the said chamber' for more than three months of a bitter winter. She and the children —11— on food brought round by her sister after dark. Christina let down a bag by a —12— from the upstairs window and her sister filled it with what she had —13—. But there was no fuel in the house and mother and children could only keep themselves warm by burning the boards of the bed and the straw from the —14—. At last a crowd of people screwed up the courage to try and rescue them. But it was no good. Payne's men had a gun mounted in a nearby house and —15— the people back. In the end Christina had to give up.

hit given nailed agreed thief brought forced business days gang mattress armed broke armour castle siege rope request refused survived

---

Section B Balcombe Street

In this section six sentences have been missed out.

☐ Read the passage carefully and try to work out what each missing sentence said.

☐ Write the number of each blank and after it write what you think that sentence should be.

Even today a family can find itself under siege. At about 9 p.m. on Saturday 6 December 1975, two shots were fired through the windows of Scott's Restaurant in London's West End. A blue car roared on down the street with four gunmen in it. Police cars were soon in pursuit. The chase was hectic, until a wrong turning took the criminals into a dead end street near Marylebone Station. They tumbled out of the car and headed for a nearby block of flats. Dashing up the stairs they knocked at the door of number 22B. ————————1— ———————————— For the next six days Mr and Mrs Matthews were to be held at gunpoint in their own flat by the four men who were in fact I.R.A. terrorists.

Grabbing food from the kitchen, the men hustled into the living room with Mr and Mrs Matthews. Then they rang the police, saying they would hold the Matthewses as hostages until some I.R.A. men imprisoned in England were released. ————————2— ———————————— The people in the flats above and below and on the opposite side of the street were moved out so that armed police could take up position. Sand bags were later piled round the flat because the police feared the terrorists might have explosives with them. They were determined to save the Matthewses but were not going to give in to the gunmen's demands.

Earlier sieges in both London and New York had taught much about how to 'fight' gunmen in situations like this. ——————— ————3———————————— Instead, the idea was to cut the enemy off from the outside world as much as possible and then start talking terms with them. The Matthewses telephone line was cut and an army field telephone was lowered down from the flat above. The gunmen could now talk to the police but no one else. Radio and television newscasters were warned to be careful what they said on the news so as not to give the police plans away. ——————— ————4———————————— All the time marksmen kept their guns trained on the windows and balcony of the flat and most of the time there was a helicopter hovering overhead. An old, engineless armoured car, owned by a neighbour as a collector's piece, was wheeled up to be used as a lookout post.

Negotiations dragged on. On Monday the gunmen threw the field telephone out of the window because the police had not sent in food. ————————————5———————————— The police would give the terrorists coffee and sandwiches when the terrorists agreed to consider releasing the lady. Meanwhile the police cut off the electricity. It was winter so the flat got really cold which depressed the gunmen as well as their hostages. At last on Thursday night they finally agreed to consider letting Mrs Matthews go. A flask of coffee with sandwiches was lowered down, the electricity was restored, and Mrs Matthews' sister went on television to make an appeal to them.

On Friday they agreed to release her and a hot meal was sent in. Then, to the surprise of the police who had expected a much longer siege, the terrorists gave in completely and came out with their hands above their heads. ————————————6————————————

Section C   A Russian school under siege

☐ Read the passage carefully and then answer the questions that follow it.

During the Second World War the German army invaded Russia. In August 1941 they reached the great city of Leningrad and besieged it. The people of Leningrad defended their city with courage and determination.

Everybody became part of this war. The men and older boys were fighting, the women and girls were in the factories making war materials, or working on the trams and buses, woodcutting or helping with civil defence and fire-fighting. The children collected scrap metal, knitted for the soldiers or delivered the soldiers' letters to their families. But school went on just the same, and the children were grateful for it.

For a start they got food at school. The army made sure the schools were supplied. Outside, in the city, during the worst weeks of winter, between ten and twenty thousand people died of starvation every day. Many children who could not get to their schools died with their families. And there was another reason why the children were glad to be in class. When the Germans were defeated, the city would need thousands of trained young people to help build the peace. So hard work at school became part of the struggle for survival. At least one headmaster noticed that his children's work was better than in normal times.

He was Mr Tikhomirov, headmaster of the secondary school in Tambov Street. His school never closed, even in the worst days of the famine. In fact it made a *Famine Scrapbook* decorated with the children's paintings of the battle scenes and filled with essays about their life during the great siege. The school was heavily shelled four times. The boys cleared up the glass, boarded up the windows with sheets of plywood and bricked up the holes in the walls. Classes went on but it was terribly hard to concentrate. In the winter the temperature was twenty degrees below freezing.

You had to be early to get a seat near the stove. 'Once you sat down you just wanted to think of nothing, only to doze off and drink in the warmth. It was agony,' Luba Tereshchenkova remembered, 'to stand up and go to the blackboard. It was so cold and dark there. Your hand in its heavy glove went numb with the cold, the chalk kept falling out of your fingers and the lines in a geometry diagram were all crooked.'

Most of the children of Tambov Street School survived the siege, but many of their teachers died. There was the lady killed by shellfire in the school yard and the Maths and Geography masters who both died of hunger. Tambov Street was just one of hundreds of Leningrad schools which had to live through the terrible months of the German siege of the city.

1 How did the younger boys help with the war effort?
2 There were two reasons why the children were grateful for school. What were they?
3 What did Mr Tikhomirov notice about the way the children worked?
4 How did the boys repair the damage when the school was shelled?
5 Why were the children keen to get to school early?
6 Why was it agony to go to the blackboard?
7 Quote two examples from the passage that show the courage of adults and children during the siege of Leningrad.

Section D   Writing

Choose one of the sieges described in this unit. Imagine that you are a child in the siege. You keep a diary describing what happens and your thoughts and feelings about it. Write what you put in your diary for one period of 24 hours.

10 THE WILD WEST

Section A   On the trail

In this section twelve words have been missed out.

☐ Read the passage through carefully and try to work out what the missing words could be.

☐ Write the numbers.

☐ Against each one write what you think that word should be.

To most people, the 'Wild West' means cowboys . . . and Texas. Texas was opened up in the 1830s. By 1860 it had —1— the 'cattle kingdom' of America. Great ranches were started in the open grasslands of the state, where thousands of longhorn —2— were bred and reared.

The cowboys who worked on these —3— worked hard and for very small wages. It was a —4— life and they had to be tough to survive. Out on the range they lived in the saddle – rounding up strays, mending —5—, fighting fires, and dealing with any other trouble that came along.

The most important job that the cowboys did was to work the trail. The cattle had to be —6— to the nearest railway. This was in Kansas, hundreds of miles away. From here the meat could be —7— to the cities of the north. There were many trails they could follow into Kansas, but the most famous was the Chisholm Trail.

The cowboys might be on the —8— for as much as four months. There were many dangers to face. There were rivers to cross. Indians or rustlers might —9— at any time. There was always the danger that the cattle might stampede. The cowboys faced all these —10— for about thirty dollars a month: little more than half the value of one cow in Chicago or New York. —11— in a single year over half a million cattle were driven along the Chisholm Trail. It is not —12— that some cowboys turned rustler, thief, or even murderer.

Section B   The Kansas cowtowns

☐ Read the passage through carefully and then answer the questions that follow it.

Where the cattle trails met the railroad in Kansas towns developed. They were the towns which first gave the west its wild name . . . Wichita, Abilene, Caldwell, Ellsworth, Dodge City.

Primitive, often little more than one wide street of wooden buildings, many with false fronts to make them more imposing in the vast spaces around them, they were built for one purpose: to receive the herds coming up from Texas. There were no pavements and thousands of wheels, boots and hooves churned the ground to knee-deep mud when it rained. In the stores that lined the streets all the necessities of life could be bought: food, clothes, hardware, guns, ammunition, saddles. There was usually a smithy, stables, barber shop, bank, and eating-houses. And cheek by jowel with these ordinary, respectable establishments – and frequently outnumbering them – were gambling houses, saloons and dance halls.

Towards this speck of civilization on the plain rode the cowboy. For perhaps eleven months of the year he was a hardworking, conscientious, sober young man. He had ridden a herd of over several thousand head of cattle for maybe fifteen hundred miles. He'd worked long hours, day and night. He'd eaten dust in the drag, and poor food when the weather turned and put out the cook's fires. He had come through the Indian territory and borne his share of danger bravely. And then suddenly, when the cattle were safely corralled at the railhead and the trail boss returned from town with the money, he found himself free. For a few weeks he had nothing to do and plenty to spend. Little wonder that he raced into town with a 'yippy' on his lips and his revolver blazing at the sky.

1   What was a false front for a shop and why did they have them?
2   Why were the streets of the towns knee-deep in mud when it rained?
3   Name three things that the shops in these towns would sell.
4   Name three other types of building, apart from shops, that you might see in these towns.
5   The buildings in the towns could be divided into two groups. What are they?
6   At the end of the passage it says, 'Little wonder that he raced into town with a 'yippy' on his lips and his revolver blazing at the sky.' Write two or three sentences explaining why it was 'little wonder' that he did this.
7   Imagine that you are a young cowboy who has just reached the end of the trail. You are paid by the trail boss and you ride into town. Write a short description of what happens during the rest of that day.

Section C   John Wesley Hardin

In this section six sentences have been missed out.

☐ Read the passage through carefully and try to work out what the six sentences must have said.
☐ Write down the numbers and after each one write what you think the sentence should be.

If the Hollywood western is to be believed, the American outlaw was a handsome and exciting hero. ————————1————— ——————— John Wesley Hardin killed a man when he was only fifteen. He had an argument with a young Negro, lost his temper, and shot him dead. Helped by his father, Hardin escaped. A posse of three men was sent after him, but Hardin ambushed them and killed all three.

Two years later, Hardin became a trail boss on the Chisholm Trail. He was driving a herd of cattle from Gonzales County in Texas up towards Abilene in Kansas. Close behind his herd was another, driven by some Mexicans. They were so close that Hardin was having great trouble keeping the two herds apart. When they reached the Little Arkansas River, Hardin's herd was forced to slow down. The two herds began to merge. Hardin rode back to speak to the Mexican trail boss. ————————————2———————————— Six Mexicans were shot dead, five of them by Hardin himself.

By the time Hardin and his men reached Abilene, news of the fight was all over town. In the weeks that followed, Hardin killed three men. The first two were shot as the result of quarrels, but the third murder was particularly vicious. Hardin was staying in a hotel in which the rooms were only separated by thin partitions. ————————————3———————————— Losing his temper, Hardin fired at the wall and shot the man dead.

Escaping on a stolen horse, Hardin returned to his home in Texas, where he still had friends to protect him. He married and became the father of two children, but still he roamed the west, gambling and quarrelling. One day in a saloon he was recognized by a deputy, who tried to shoot him. ————————————4———————————— This was his 39th victim.

Hardin went on the run, with his wife and children. For a few years he travelled from state to state, trying to avoid capture. Eventually the Texas Rangers caught up with him. He was travelling by train and the rangers trapped him in the middle of a carriage. He struggled to draw his gun, but it became entangled in his braces and at last Hardin was caught. ————————————5———————————— After serving fifteen of them he was freed on the orders of the State Governor.

While in prison, Hardin had studied the law. Now he passed the necessary examinations and set up as a lawyer in El Paso. ————————————6———————————— He was soon back at his old pastimes of gambling, drinking, and quarrelling. As the result of one such quarrel he was finally shot – in the back, by a rustler turned policeman.

Section D   Writing

You are the Editor of the 'El Paso Times'. You decide to bring out a special edition about the death of Hardin. It contains a front page story, with headline, describing how he died. Inside there is an article about Hardin's life and career. Write the front page story and the article inside the paper.

11 CHUNNY'S PIG

Section A Preparations

In this section ten words have been missed out. There is a list of thirty words at the end of the passage and the ten missing words are included in this list.

☐ Read the passage and choose words from the list to fit the blanks.

☐ Write down the numbers of the blanks and the words you have chosen.

Every Monday I went pig-killing with my Dad and my Uncle Dick.

You see everybody in our village kept a pig. If you were poor you shared a pig with a —1—. When the pig was cut up you used to pack salt round it in a big wooden trough and after a few weeks you hung the bits of pig all round the living room walls. They were like pictures nowadays, except you kept —2— bits off to keep you going through the winter.

In case you don't know how to —3— a pig, I'll tell you. At about eight o'clock on Monday morning we would set off in our old green Commer van, Uncle Dick driving, my Dad in the passenger seat smoking Digger Flake and me sitting in the scalding tub in the back of the van surrounded by knives, scrapers, skewers and the cratch – all the —4— needed to kill a pig. The first thing you do when you arrive is to check that they've got the copper boiling. You need about ten buckets of —5— water to kill a pig, and if the copper isn't boiling my Uncle Dick gets mad.

I remember when we went to kill Chunny James's pig one year and her water wasn't even warm. Uncle Dick stomped round Chunny's yard in his Wellington boots smoking his Craven A fags and wiping his nose on his apron – he always wore a blue apron for killing a pig. Anyway he'd smoked five fags before the copper boiled; it took him a long time to smoke a fag too because he used to stick a —6— in the end so he could smoke every shred of tobacco.

When the copper was boiling at last, my Dad and me went to catch Chunny's pig. Chunny's sty was at the bottom of her garden so we thought we'd kill the pig near the sty and carry it back to the yard on the cratch – the cratch was like the —7— you see them carrying people who have fainted out of football grounds, only bigger, because pigs are bigger than people I suppose.

Chunny's pig was a sixteen-stoner with a black stripe down its back. I knew it would take a lot of killing as soon as I saw it and the black stripe was a —8— too. Black bristles took much more —9— off than white ones.

As soon as we looked over the sty at Chunny's pig, it stood up, grunted and went through the hole at the end of its sty into the small section where it —10—.

'See if you can get the rope on it, boy. If you can't, just drive it out.'

television   cold   nuisance   assassinate   stretcher   pity   guns
policeman   tackle   brother   wiping   pin   ambulance   neighbour
beauty   kill   courage   died   cutting   butcher   cutting   enemy
boiling   went   lukewarm   heaving   stick   slept   scraping   finger

Section B   The killing

This section has been divided into eight parts. Except for the first, the other parts have been printed in the wrong order.

☐ Read them through and decide what the correct order should be.

☐ Write the numbers in that order.

I was only about seven so I could get through the hole easily. Chunny's pig was sitting on its straw looking a bit fierce. The rope was about ten feet long with a loop at the end. You had to get the loop between its teeth – like a bit in a horse's mouth – and then pull it tight. I crawled up to the pig and slowly dangled the loop on its snout. It did a very stupid thing then, did Chunny's pig. It bit at the loop and that was just what I wanted and I pulled the rope tight. It got up and pulled me through the gap into the main part of the sty. I probably looked like a midget trying to take an Alsatian for a walk.

1 It was wooden and shaped like a half-barrel but about four feet across and two feet deep with tar on the outside to stop the water running out. By the time Dad and Dick arrived with the pig I'd already got the first two buckets of boiling water in the scalding trough.

Ten buckets of water in the tub and in went the pig's head and shoulders.

2 As soon as I pulled on the rope Chunny's pig started screaming like a . . . well I've never heard anything scream half so loud as a stuck pig.

It seemed that one second there was Uncle Dick's black hairy bare arm with a clean shining knife in his hand and the next second everything was covered in blood. Dick's arm and apron and even his Wellington boots were thick red.

3 We got our knives out then and scraped off the rest of the hairs, dipping our knives in the water every now and then to clean them. When Uncle Dick was satisfied that there were no more hairs to cut off – I'd cut through its skin twice trying to get the black hairs out of its back and Dick scowled at me and I thought he was going to clip my ear – we put the pig on its back on the cratch and tied its back legs to the handles. Then we propped it up, head down, against the wall of Chunny's house.

4 'Good lad', said my Dad when he saw I was still holding the rope. I didn't tell him it was a fluke. Then we walked the pig round the side of the sty where we were going to kill it.

Well, we pushed Chunny's pig against the wall of the sty and my

Dad got hold of its tail in his left hand and pushed his whole weight against its body so it couldn't back away. My job was to pull its head up with the rope and as soon as I'd done this Uncle Dick cut its throat with a quick upward thrust of his nine-inch knife.

5 You could test it by putting a trickle of boiling water in its ear. If it didn't flap its ear it was dead.

Then we rolled the pig on the cratch and I took the bloodied rope from its mouth. Uncle Dick and Dad then staggered up the path carrying the pig and I ran on to get the scalding trough as near to the copper as I could. I set it up outside Chunny's back door.

6 Then we picked up our scrapers and worked like madmen. A scraper looks like a big mushroom but with a sharp metal rim round the top. We scraped away at Chunny's pig, the hairs coming away in wet lumps. After about two minutes we turned the pig over and scraped the other side; then turned it round and put its behind in the water.

In about ten minutes the pig was on the cratch looking quite clean.

7 We held the pig upright till most of its blood was gone. At least Chunny didn't stand around holding basins and tins to catch the blood to make black puddings like some of them did. That was always a nuisance – they used to get in your way.

The screaming gave way to grunts and Chunny's pig flopped on to its side; but it wasn't dead yet. You had to pump the rest of the blood out of the hole in its throat by lifting its fore-leg up and down. My Dad did this for a bit and in about five minutes the pig was properly dead.

Section C   Clearing up

☐ Read the passage and then answer the questions that follow.

Uncle Dick slit the pig from top to bottom with his killing knife and took out its insides. He staggered off with his arms full of pig's guts and dropped them all in the scalding tub – I'd tipped the water and hair away down Chunny's drain. Dick then cut out the liver and heart and dropped them into a clean bucket of water; this was pig's fry and Chunny might give us a bit to take back for our suppers.

I knew what my job was now and I didn't like it. There was about three miles of pig's intestines in the scalding tub and I had to find the end and run the whole lot through my fingers. I didn't mind it too much until I got near the end. Then all the pig muck started coming out over my boots and it used to stink something horrible. It had to be done though because we needed the insides to make sausages with – we had them properly cleaned though before we put sausage meat in them.

When I'd finished that nasty job I had to go and pull the pig's toe nails off with a metal hook. Sometimes you could hurt yourself doing that; you'd get the hook in the nail and pull and pull and suddenly it would give and over you'd go smack on your backside.

I managed to do it easy though with Chunny's pig and when I'd finished my jobs I went to my Dad and asked him for the bladder. Uncle Dick had just finished cutting off its head and he dropped it upside down in another bucket. My Dad had saved me the bladder and I blew it up and tied the end with a piece of binder-twine.

Then I played football with it round Chunny's yard till it burst – they didn't last long. When I got back I was just in time to help swill down. We chucked a few buckets of cold water over the pig and washed the rest of the blood and hair down the drain. My Dad loaded the tackle in the van and I buried the rest of the insides in the garden while Dick went to get the money from Chunny.

Anyway that's how we killed Chunny's pig and that's how we killed hundreds of pigs when I was a boy. I hope you didn't think it was cruel the way we killed pigs. I certainly would do now but I didn't think about it then; I just grew up with it, I suppose.

1 Did you find reading this story – the whole story – unpleasant, interesting, unusual . . . or what?
2 What were the reasons for your feelings about the story?
3 If you had been the person telling the story, which part would you have liked least and why?
4 Some people dislike reading about this kind of thing, yet they enjoy eating meat. What do you think of this attitude and why?
5 What kind of person do you think Chunny was, and why?

Section D   Writing

These days few people keep a pig of their own and have it slaughtered in this way. Yet even fifty years ago it was quite common. Think of a custom that is common nowadays but will probably have died out in fifty years' time. Write a story about it, as if you were looking back on your childhood, aged about sixty.

12 KILL TO EAT

Section A Stradbroke

In this section a number of sentences have been missed out. They are listed at the end of the section, in the wrong order.

☐ Read the passage and decide which sentence should fill which space.

☐ Write the number of each space, and against it write the letter of the sentence you have chosen.

Years ago, my family – my Aboriginal family – lived on Stradbroke Island. Years before the greedy mineral seekers came to scar the landscape and break the back of this lovely island. I recall how we used to make the trip to Point Lookout. My father would saddle our horses at early light and we would make our way along the shoreline, then cut inland to climb over the hills covered with flowering pines, wattles and gums. The brumbies would watch our approach from a safe distance. These wild horses never trusted man, their foe. ———

————————1————————

The shells washed up by the sea delighted us. ————————

————————2———————————— Father told us that some of our neighbours to the north of Australia prayed to their god to bless their fishing fleet, and tossed these model ships into the sea to appease the waves.

There was one sight we loved above all others. When we arrived at Point Lookout, we would tether our horses out of sight, then take up position behind the small sandhills that dotted the shore. We would lie full-length upon our stomachs and silently wait for the beautiful nautilus shells to come out of the sea. ———————————3—

———————————— Their trumpet-like shells would unfurl to the breeze a sail, mauve-coloured, which caught the sun's rays and shone like satin. We feasted our eyes upon the sight, knowing it would not last long, for at the least sound these shy creatures would immediately draw in their satin sails and drop like stones to the safety of the sea bottom.

———————————4——————————————— Civilization and man's greed have chased away our shy nautilus shells. Motor-cars belch fumes over the land, and the noise of industry drowns out all other sounds of life. Men's machines have cut and maimed and destroyed what used to be.

———————————5——————————— The birds and animals are going. The trees and flowers are being pushed aside and left to die. Tourists come to soak up the sunshine and bathe in the blue Pacific, scattering as they go their discarded cans and cigarette packs and bottles and even the hulks of cars.

Greedy, thoughtless, stupid, ignorant man continues the assault on nature. But he too will suffer. ———————————6———————

My father worked for the Government, as ganger of an Aboriginal workforce which helped to build roads, load and unload the supply ships, and carry out all the menial tasks around the island. ———————————7——————————— (I was the third-eldest daughter.) We hated the white man's rations – besides, they were so meagre that even a bandicoot would have had difficulty in existing on them. They used to include meat, rice, sago, tapioca, and on special occasions, such as the Queen's Birthday festival, one plum pudding.

a) They looked like little ships in full sail.
b) For this work he received a small wage and rations to feed his seven children.
c) They would nuzzle their foals, warning them to stay away from danger.
d) The island is different now.

e) His ruthless bulldozers are digging his own grave.
f) Stradbroke is dying.
g) Sometimes, too, we found strange, small-scale outrigger craft.

Section B Hunting

☐ Read the passage and then follow the instructions at the end.

Of course, we never depended upon the rations to keep ourselves alive. Dad taught us how to catch our food Aboriginal-style, using discarded materials from the white man's rubbish dumps. We each had our own sling-shots to bring down the blueys and greenies – the parrots and lorikeets that haunted the flowering gums. And he showed us how to make bandicoot traps; a wooden box, a bit of wire, a lever on top and a piece of burnt toast were all that was needed. Bandicoots cannot resist burnt toast. We would set our traps at dusk, and always next day there was a trapped-bandicoot to take proudly home for Mother to roast. Dad also showed us how to flatten a square piece of tin and sharpen it. This was very valuable for slicing through the shallow waters; many a mullet met its doom from the accurate aim of one of my brothers wielding the sharpened tin. Dad made long iron crab hooks, too, and we each had a hand fishing-line of our own.

One rule he told us we must strictly obey. When we went hunting, we must understand that our weapons were to be used only for the gathering of food. We must never use them for the sake of killing. This is in fact one of the strictest laws of the Aborigine, and no excuse is accepted for abusing it.

One day we five children, two boys and three girls, decided to follow the noise of the blueys and greenies screeching from the flowering gums. We armed ourselves with our sling-shots and made our way towards the trees.

My sisters and I always shot at our quarry from the ground. The boys would climb onto the branches of the gum-trees, stand quite still, and pick out the choicest and healthiest birds in the flock. My elder brother was by far the best shot of all of us. He was always boasting about it, too. But never in front of our mother and father, because he would have been punished for his vanity. He only boasted in front of us, knowing that we wouldn't complain about him to our parents.

The boys ordered us to take up our positions under the trees as quietly as possible. 'Don't make so much noise!' they told us. In spite of the disgust we felt for our boastful brother, we always let him start the shooting. He was a dead shot, and we all knew it. Now we watched as he drew a bead on the large bluey straight across from him. The bird seemed intent on its honey-gathering from the gum-tree. We held our breath and our brother fired.

Suddenly there was a screeching from the birds and away they flew, leaving my brother as astonished as we were ourselves. He had been so close to his victim that it seemed impossible he should have missed . . . but he had. We looked at him, and his face of blank disbelief was just too much for us. We roared with laughter. My other brother jumped to the ground and rolled over and over, laughing his head off. But the more we laughed, the angrier my elder brother became.

1 Copy and complete this table:

QUARRY	HUNTING METHOD	WEAPON MADE FROM
		wooden box, wire
		sharpened tin
	sling-shot	- - - -
crabs		

2 The main part of this section tells the beginning of a story. Make a numbered list of the main events in the story. Begin like this:

1. We decided to go hunting blueys and greenies.
2. We got our sling-shots
3.

3 The passage describes the boy who was chosen to have the first shot at the birds. It gives two kinds of information about him – facts and opinions. For example:

He was the elder brother : FACT
We felt disgust for him : OPINION

Make a list of all the facts about him, and another list of all the opinions.

Section C Kookaburra

☐ Read the passage and answer the questions that follow it.

Then, seeming to join in the fun, a kookaburra in a nearby tree started his raucous chuckle, which rose to full pitch just as though he, too, saw the joke.

In anger my elder brother brought up his sling-shot and fired blindly at the sound. 'Laugh at me, would you!' he called out. He hadn't even taken time to aim.

Our laughter was cut short by the fall of the kookaburra to the ground. My brother, horrified, his anger gone, climbed down and we gathered silently around the stricken bird. That wild aim had broken the bird's wing beyond repair. We looked at each other in frightened silence, knowing full well what we had done. We had broken that strict rule of the Aboriginal law. We had killed for the sake of killing – and we had destroyed a bird we were forbidden to destroy. The Aborigine does not eat the kookaburra. His merry laughter is allowed to go unchecked, for he brings happiness to the tribes. We call him our brother and friend.

We did not see our father coming towards us. He must have been looking for firewood. When he came upon us, we parted to allow him to see what had happened. He checked his anger by remaining silent and picking up a fallen branch. Mercifully he put the stricken bird out of its misery. Then he ordered us home.

On the way back we talked with awesome foreboding of the punishment we knew would come. I wished our father would beat us, but we all knew it would not be a quick punishment. Besides, Dad never beat us. No, we knew the punishment would be carefully weighed to fit the crime. When we got home, our mother was told to give us our meal. Nothing was said of the dead kookaburra, but we knew Dad would broach the subject after we had eaten. None of us felt hungry, and our mother only played with her food. We knew that Dad had decided upon the punishment, and that Mother had agreed to it, even if she felt unhappy about it.

It was our mother who ordered us to bring into the backyard our bandicoot traps, our sling-shots, and every other weapon we had. We had to place them in a heap in the yard, while our father carefully checked every item. Our big black dog stood with us. He always did that when there was trouble in the family. Although he could not possibly understand the ways of human beings, he could nevertheless interpret an atmosphere of trouble when it came.

Father spoke for the first time since we had killed the kookaburra. He asked for no excuses for what we had done, and we did not offer any. We must all take the blame. That is the way of the Aborigine. Since we had killed for the sake of killing, the punishment was that for three months we should not hunt or use our weapons. For three months we would eat only the white man's hated rations.

During those three months our stomachs growled, and our puzzled dog would question with his eyes and wagging tail why we sat around wasting our time when there was hunting to be done.

It happened a long time ago. Yet in my dreams, the sad, suffering eyes of the kookaburra, our brother and friend, still haunt me.

1 What mood was the elder brother in *before* the kookaburra started laughing, and why?
2 How did he react to the bird's laughter?
3 Which word in the passage describes his feelings when he saw what he had done?
4 He knew he had done wrong. Exactly *what* had he done wrong?
5 Why was their father near them at the time?
6 Why did their father kill the kookaburra?
7 What did their mother do when they got home?
8 Why did they have to pile up all their weapons?
9 Why didn't their father just punish the elder brother and leave the rest of them alone?
10 How long did the punishment last?

The questions that follow require more thought and longer answers.

11 When the children got home there was a period of time *before* their father told them their punishment. What was the atmosphere? How do you know?
12 The passage refers to a number of Aboriginal laws and customs. Make a list of all those you can find.

Section D Writing

This story describes a way of life that has now largely disappeared. What do you think has been lost? Has anything been gained? Think about these questions and then write down your opinions. In your answer refer to the story in as much detail as possible.

13 FIRE

Wallace, Graham, and Harry are camping in the Australian outback. They have a tent, sleeping bags, cooking pots, and a stove that works by methylated spirits. It is night. It is very hot and dry.

Section A   Coffee

In this section ten words have been changed. The new word either does not make sense, or it is not as good as the old word.

- ☐ Read the passage carefully and find the words that are wrong or unsuitable.
- ☐ Write these words down.
- ☐ Beside each one write a word that you think would be more suitable.

Wallace was half-awake, half-awake. He had been asleep for a while, but had become partly aware of his surroundings again, of the wind and the cold. He was wet with perspiration. Graham had been right about sleeping bags and ovens. Wallace felt that he was being cooked

5 and his right eye was bruised and sore. He had dug a little hole for his hip, but he must have turned away from it. The usual was, he couldn't completely wake up. He was in a sort of limbo of very discomfort but was too hazy in the head to do anything about it.

When at last he managed to open his eyes he became aware of a
10 faint glow. He thought he could hear methylated spirits. He perhaps thought he could see Graham.

'Is that you?' he said.

'Yes,' said Graham.

'What are you doing?'

15 'Making coffee.'

Wallace sat up, puffing. He felt giddy. 'What are you making coffee for?'

'I'm hungry. Do you want a cup?'

'What's the time?'

20 'Twenty past one.'

'Yeh. I'll take a cup.'

Section B Methylated spirits

This section has been divided into eight parts. Except for the first one, all the parts have been printed in the wrong order.

☐ Read the section through carefully and decide what you think the correct order of the parts is.

☐ Write down the numbers in that order.

Wallace peeled his sleeping bag down to the waist, and felt better.
'Twenty past one!'

'About that.'

'Harry's sleepin' all right.'

1   'How could it come out? Honest to goodness –'

'It's *burning*,' howled Graham.

A blue flame snaked from the little heater up through the rocks towards the bottle in the boy's hand; or at least that was how it seemed to happen. It happened so swiftly it may have deceived the eye. Instinctively, to protect himself, Graham threw the bottle away.

2   'Can't see when it boils if you've got the lid on.'
       'Put the lid on, I reckon, or it'll never boil.'
       'Don't know where the lid is, do you?'
       '*Feel* for it. It's there somewhere. Use your torch.'

3   It was so quick. It was terrible.
       'Put it out,' cried Graham, and Harry fought out of his sleeping
       bag, knowing somehow that they'd never get it out by beating at it,
       that they'd have to get water up from the creek. But all they had was a
       four pint billycan.

4   'Trust Harry,' said Graham. 'He could sleep anywhere.'
       Wallace thought he'd heard something like that before, but
       couldn't remember when. 'Funny in the bush at night, isn't it? Awful
       dark.'
       'Noisy, too. I heard a tree fall down. Not far away either. Woke me
       up.'

5   There was a shower of fire from its neck, as from the nozzle of a
       hose.
       'Oh my gosh,' yelled Wallace and tore off his sleeping bag.
       'Harry!' he screamed. 'Wake up, Harry!'
       They tried to stamp on the fire, but their feet were bare and they
       couldn't find their shoes. They tried to smother it with their sleeping
       bags, but it seemed to be everywhere.
       'Put it out,' shouted Graham. 'Put it out.'
       It wasn't dark any longer. It was a flickering world of tree trunks
       and twisted boughs, of scrub and saplings and stones, of shouts and
       wind and smoke and frantic fear.

6   'The battery's flat. Blooming thing. Must have been a crook
       battery. Hardly used it all. *Now* look what I've done! There's the
       metho bottle knocked for six.'
       'You dope,' cried Wallace. 'Pick it up quick. Or we'll lose it all.'
       'The cork's in it.' Graham groped for it, feeling a bit of a fool, and
       said, 'Crumbs.'
       'Now what?'
       'The cork's *not* in it, that's what. It must have come out.'

7   'It's the wind.'
     'Guess so.'
     'Stinkin' hot, isn't it?'
     'You can say that again. But this water's awful slow coming to the boil.'
     'The wind, I suppose.'
     'It's taken two lots of metho already,' said Graham.
     'Have you got the lid on?'

Section C   Fire

Five sentences, or parts of sentences, have been missed out in this section.

☐ Read the passage and work out what the sentences must have been.

☐ Write the number of each blank and against it what you think that sentence should be.

The fire was getting away from them in all directions, crackling through the scrub downwind, burning fiercely back into the wind. Even the ground burned; ――――――――――1――――――――
―――― There were flames on the trees, bark was burning, foliage was flaring, flaring like a whipcrack; and the heat was savage and searing and awful to breathe.
     'We can't, we can't,' cried Wallace. 'What are we going to do?'
     They beat at it and beat at it and beat at it.
     'Oh gee,' sobbed Graham. He was crying, and he hadn't cried since he was twelve years old. 'What have I done? *We've got to get it out!*'
     They were blackened, their feet were cut, even their hair was singed. They beat and beat, and fire was leaping into the treetops, and there were no black shadows left, only bright light, red light, yellow light, light that was hard and cruel and terrifying, and there was a rushing sound, a roaring sound, explosions and smoke, smoke like a hot red fog.
     'No,' cried Graham. 'No, no, no.' ――――――――――2――――
―――――――― 'Oh, Wally,' he sobbed. 'What have I done?'
     'We've got to get out of here,' shouted Harry. 'Grab the things and run.'
     'Our shoes?' cried Wallace. 'Where are they?'
     'I don't know. I don't know.'
     'We've got to find our shoes.'

'They'll kill us,' sobbed Graham. 'They'll kill us. It's a terrible thing, an awful thing to have done.'

'Where'd we put our shoes?' Wallace was running around in circles, blindly. ————————————3————————————
Everything had happened so quickly, so suddenly.

'For Pete's sake run!' shouted Harry.

Something in his voice seemed to get through to Wallace and Graham and they ran, the three of them, like frightened rabbits. They ran this way and that hugging their packs and their scorched sleeping bags, blundering into the scrub, even into the trunks of trees. ————————————4———————————— The fire's rays darted through the bush; it was like an endless chain with a will of its own, encircling and entangling them, or like a wall that leaped out of the earth to block every fresh run they made for safety. Even the creek couldn't help them. They didn't know where it was. There might as well not have been a creek at all.

'This way,' shouted Harry. 'A track.'

They stumbled back down the track towards Tinley; ——————
————————————5———————————— Perhaps they were running to save their lives, running simply from fear, running away from what they had done.

When they thought they were safe they hid in the bush close to a partly constructed house. They could hear sirens wailing; lights were coming on here and there; the headlamps of cars were beaming and sweeping around curves in the track. They could hear shouts on the wind, they heard a woman cry hysterically, they heard Graham sobbing. Over all was a red glow.

Section D Writing

1 'They'll kill us,' sobbed Graham . . . 'It's a terrible thing . . . to have done.' Explain why it is such a terrible thing and what the boys did wrong.
2 What do you think happened next? Write the next part of the story.

14 THE ANT WAR

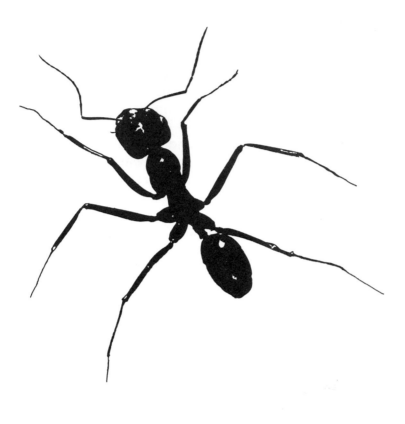

Section A   Finding the nest

In this section ten words have been missed out.

☐ Read the passage through and work out what the missing words should be.

☐ Write the number of each blank and beside it write the word you have chosen.

I remember once lying on a sun-drenched hillside in Greece – a hillside covered with twisted olive-trees and myrtle bushes – and watching a protracted and bloody war being —1— within inches of my feet. I was extremely lucky to be, as it were, war correspondent for this battle. It was the only one of its —2— I have ever seen and I would not have missed it for the world.

The two armies involved were ants. The —3— force was a shining, fierce red, while the defending army was as black as —4—. I might quite easily have missed this if one day I had not noticed what struck me as an extremely peculiar ants' nest. It contained two species of —5—, one red and one black, living together on the most amicable terms. Never having seen two species of ants living in the same nest before, I took the trouble to check up on them, and discovered that the —6— ones, who were the true owners of the nest, were known by the resounding title of the blood-red slave-makers, and the —7— ones were in fact their slaves who had been captured and placed in their service while they were still eggs. After reading about the habits of the slave-makers, I kept a cautious —8— on the nest in the hope of seeing them indulge in one of their slave raids. Several months —9— and I began to think that either these slave-makers were too lazy or else they had enough —10— to keep them happy.

Section B The battle begins

This section has been divided into eight parts. The first part has been printed at the beginning. The remaining seven parts have been jumbled up.

☐ Read the section through and decide what the correct order of the parts should be.

☐ Write the numbers in that order.

The slave-makers' fortress lay near the roots of an olive-tree, and some thirty feet farther down the hillside was a nest of black ants. Passing this nest one morning, I noticed several of the slave-makers wandering about within a yard or so of it, and I stopped to watch. There were perhaps thirty or forty of them, spread over quite a large area. They did not appear to be foraging for food, as they were not moving with their normal brisk inquisitiveness.

1   Then I arrived one morning to find that the war had started.
      The scouts, accompanied by four or five small platoons, had now moved in closer to the black ants, and already several skirmishes were taking place within two or three feet of the nest. Black ants were hurling themselves on the red ones with almost hysterical fervour, while the red ones were advancing slowly but inexorably, now and then catching a black ant and with a swift, savage bite piercing it through the head or the thorax with their huge jaws.

2   I was torn between a desire to help the black ants in some way and a longing to leave things as they were and see how matters developed. I did pick up one of the black ants and place him near the encircling red-ant column, but he was set upon and killed rapidly, and I felt quite guilty.

3   Occasionally one of them would meet one of the slave-makers and would turn tail and run back to the nest to join one of the many groups of his relatives who were gathered in little knots, apparently holding a council of war. This careful investigation of the ground by the scouts of the slave-makers' army continued for two days, and I had begun to think that they had decided the black ants' city was too difficult to attack.

4   They kept wandering round in vague circles, occasionally climbing a grass blade and standing pensively on its tip, waving their antennae. Periodically, two of them would meet and stand there in what appeared to be animated conversation, their antennae twitching together. It was not until I had watched them for some time that I realized what they were doing. Their wanderings were not as aimless as they appeared, for they were quartering the ground very thoroughly like a pack of hunting-dogs, investigating every bit of the terrain over which their army would have to travel. The black ants seemed distinctly ill at ease.

5   I could see the columns of reinforcements hurrying up through the jungle of grass; see the two outflanking columns of slave-makers moving nearer and nearer to the nest, while the black ants, unaware of their presence, were concentrating on fighting off the central column. It was quite obvious to me that unless the black ants very soon realized that they were being encircled, they had lost all hope of survival.

6   While one column marched directly on the nest the other two spread out and proceeded to execute a flanking or pincer movement. It was fascinating to watch. I felt I was suspended in some miraculous way above the field of battle of some old military campaign – the battle of Waterloo or some similar historic battle. I could see at a glance the disposition of the attackers and the defenders;

7   Half-way up the hillside the main body of the slave-makers' army was marching down. In about an hour they had got within four or five feet of the black ants' city, and here, with a beautiful military precision which was quite amazing to watch, they split into three columns.

Section C   Victory and defeat

☐ Read the passage through and then answer the questions that follow it.

Eventually, however, the black ants suddenly became aware of the fact that they were being neatly surrounded. Immediately they seemed to panic; numbers of them ran to and fro aimlessly, some of them in their fright running straight into the red invaders and being instantly killed. Others, however, seemed to keep their heads, and they rushed down into the depths of the fortress and started on the work of evacuating the eggs, which they brought up and stacked on the side of nest farthest away from the invaders. Other members of the community then seized the eggs and started to rush them away to safety. But they had left it too late.

The encircling columns of slave-makers, so orderly and neat, now suddenly burst their ranks and spread over the whole area, like a scuttling red tide. Everywhere there were knots of struggling ants. Black ones, clasping eggs in their jaws, were pursued by the slave-makers, cornered and then forced to give up the eggs. If they showed fight, they were immediately killed; the more cowardly, however, saved their lives by dropping the eggs they were carrying as soon as a slave-maker hove in sight. The whole area on and around the nest was littered with dead and dying ants of both species, while between the corpses the black ants ran futilely hither and thither, and the slave-makers gathered the eggs and started on the journey back to their fortress on the hill. At that point, very reluctantly, I had to leave the scene of battle, for it was getting too dark to see properly.

Early next morning I arrived at the scene again, to find the war was over. The black ants' city was deserted, except for the dead and injured ants littered all over it. Neither the black nor the red army were anywhere to be seen. I hurried up to the red ants' nest and was just in time to see the last of the army arrive there, carrying their spoils of war, the eggs, carefully in their jaws. At the entrance to the nest their black slaves greeted them excitedly, touching the eggs with their antennae and scuttling eagerly around their masters, obviously full of enthusiasm for the successful raid on their own relations that the slave-makers had achieved. There was something unpleasantly human about the whole thing.

1 When the black ants realized they were being attacked, they reacted in two main ways. What were they?
2 What did the columns of red ants do as they reached the black ants' nest?
3 Some of the black ants tried to save the eggs. What happened to those which were brave?
4 What did the cowardly ones do?
5 Why did the writer stop watching?
6 What did the black ants' nest look like the next day?
7 How did the slaves react to the red ants' victory?
8 What is the meaning of the last sentence?

Section D Writing

This description of the battle between the ants is written in a personal way; it is like a story that actually happened to the author. It is a very different style from that normally used in natural history or biology textbooks. Imagine that you were writing such a textbook. You have to give a short, simple, and *clear* account of how the red ants attack the black ants and steal their eggs. Write your account in no more than a hundred words and draw a diagram to illustrate it.

15 HUNTERS AND HUNTED

Section A   Plains game

☐ Read the passage through and then answer the questions that follow on pages 75–76.

In parts of East Africa there still occur spectacular concentrations of big animals such as no longer exist anywhere else in the world. The most famous of the concentrations is found within the Serengeti National Park in north western Tanzania and in the adjoining Mara Game Reserve in Kenya. Here over a million head of game live in 2000 square kilometres of undulating plains interspersed with acacia woodland and riverine forest. There are many thousands of wildebeestes, zebras, topis and gazelles, but also numerous giraffes, black rhinoceroses, elands and other antelopes large and small of over twenty species. The grasslands of East Africa are able to support this great variety and profusion of large herbivores because almost all the species are separated ecologically, some by their food requirements, some by their preferences for different types of grassland.

Grazers and browsers

The animals listed above can be divided into *grazers* and *browsers*:

browser

grazer

Even amongst the grazers, different animals have different requirements. Not only does this mean that they eat different parts of the
grass plant but they actually help each other out.

1 **Zebra**

Strong, sharp teeth
Good digestion
Ability to extract nourishment
from low grade material
Eat outside of tough stem

2 **Topi**

Pointed muzzle

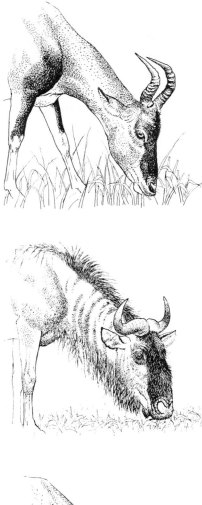

3 **Wildebeeste**

Square muzzle

4 **Thomson's Gazelle**

Earlier cropping by the other animals encourages new growth from the base of the plant.

1 Without using a dictionary, write your own definition of the words *grazer* and *browser*. Look the two words up in a dictionary and compare the dictionary definition with your own.
2 Make a list of any other words in the passage that you do not know the meaning of. Where possible have a guess at their meaning. Look them all up in a dictionary.

3 Explain in your own words why the Serengeti National Park is famous.
4 How many different species are to be found there?
5 The sentence that begins 'The grasslands of East Africa . . .' explains why it is possible for so many animals to live together in such an area. What reason does it give?
6 The four pictures at the end of the passage show how four different animals 'actually help each other out'. Study them carefully and then write your own explanation of how this happens.

Section B   The hunters

☐ Read the passage and then answer the questions that follow.

In order to catch the grazers, the predators on the plain have had to improve greatly their own running techniques. They have effectively lengthened their limbs:

The cheetah has a thin elongated body and is said to be the fastest runner on earth, capable of reaching speeds, in bursts, of over 110 kph. But this method is very energy-consuming. Great muscular effort is needed to keep the spine springing back and forth and the cheetah cannot maintain such speeds for more than a minute or so. Either it succeeds in outrunning its prey within a few hundred yards and makes a kill or it has to retire exhausted while the antelope, with their more rigid back and long lever-legs continue to gallop off to a safer part of the plains.

Lions are nowhere near as fast as the cheetah. Their top speed is about 80 kph. A wildebeest can do about the same and keep it up for much longer. So lions have had to develop more complicated tactics. Sometimes they rely on stealth, creeping towards their victims, their bodies close to the ground, utilizing every bit of cover. Sometimes, an individual works by itself. But on occasion, members of a pride will hunt as a team – and they are the only cats that do so. They set off in line abreast. As they approach a group of their prey – antelope, zebra or wildebeest – those lions at the ends of the line move a little quicker so that they encircle the herd. Finally these break cover, driving the prey towards the lions in the centre of the line. Such tactics often result in several of the team making kills and a hunt has been watched in which seven wildebeest were brought down.

1 When a cheetah hunts an antelope, what advantage does the cheetah have?
2 What advantages does the antelope have?
3 Why cannot a lion just chase after a wildebeest, overtake it and kill it?
4 How exactly does a lion 'rely on stealth'?

These questions require careful reading and thought before answering:

5 The second sentence says that the predators have 'effectively lengthened their limbs.' Study the pictures carefully and then explain what you think this sentence means.
6 Draw a sequence of diagrams to show how a group of lions acts as a team to hunt. You may use labels, but don't use any sentences to explain your drawings.

Section C   Ecology

☐ Study the diagram opposite, read the text and then answer the
questions that follow.

Grasshoppers, grass-eating rodents (shown here by the grass rat and
the African hare) and plains game large and small are the bases of
the three great food pyramids of the plains. Most grass-eaters are
preyed on by either insect-eaters or by carnivores; carnivores may
eat the insect-eaters and the carnivores may in turn be eaten by
larger carnivores. Only the great super-predators and scavengers
at the summit of the pyramid are free from the threat of predation.

1   Draw a simpler diagram to illustrate the food pyramid of which
the vagrant hedgehog is a part.
2   Make a list of the 'super-predators and scavengers' that 'are free
from the threat of predation'.
3   Study the diagram carefully and then write a paragraph explaining what is meant by a food pyramid.

Section D   Writing

After reading this unit, do you think that nature is cruel? Write an
explanation of your thoughts about this, giving the reasons for what
you think.

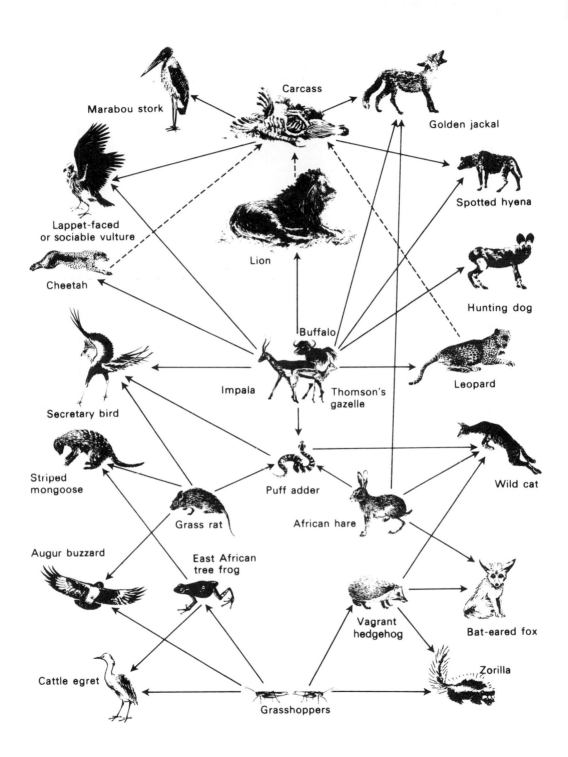

Marabou stork

Carcass

Golden jackal

Lappet-faced
or sociable vulture

Spotted hyena

Cheetah

Lion

Hunting dog

Buffalo

Secretary bird

Impala

Thomson's
gazelle

Leopard

Striped
mongoose

Puff adder

African hare

Wild cat

Grass rat

Augur buzzard

East African
tree frog

Vagrant
hedgehog

Bat-eared fox

Cattle egret

Zorilla

Grasshoppers

The web of life in grassland

16 SEARCHING FOR WATER

Section A   Setting off

☐ Read the passage through carefully and then answer the questions that follow it.

At around four o'clock, about an hour and a half before dawn on the following morning, Wednesday, the wives of the four close families met on the Nain main road, near the post office, and set out briskly to collect their household stores of water, as they had arranged the afternoon before in the market.

Miriam was carrying a large kerosene tin and a bucket. Quasheba and Beneba were both pushing small hand-carts with an assortment of pots and pans jangling in them. And Juba was swinging two demijohns. Their plan was that after they had found a suitable stream, they would then make three or four trips to it, until they had filled the empty asphalt drums in their kitchens.

The morning was already very warm. As the women hurried along the road they could smell the dying fragrance of the night blooms and they could begin to detect the usual invasion of the dry, acrid day-smells: the burning of pitch pine in early fires, the dregs of drawn coffee and the sourness of the yeast used in the home-made bread, the stale scent of the uncultivated family plots and the abandoned yam hills, the overlay of the rising dust on the high banks at the sides of the road, and more.

As soon as they had left the main road and crossed into the first open field, the women began to sing. They sang Methodist hymns which were familiar and dear to them. They sang all the way up to the first stream they came to. Had their husbands come along they would have wanted to dictate the choice of the hymns, but as it turned out the women had volunteered to fetch the water, and so they were free to sing whatever they chose.

They were standing together and gazing disappointedly at the stream.

'Too dirty,' was Miriam's decision, as she backed away from it.

'Look to me as if Simeon an' them other little devils been playin' in it, yes,' Juba agreed, laughing gently.

'Not only your Simeon but me own Jeremiah too,' Beneba suggested.

'An' you can count in Joshua,' Quasheba said, leaning over her hand-cart and picking up a pot cover and slamming it down.

To which Miriam quickly added, 'Seth an' the whole o' Nain School.'

They turned away and figured where next to go. They decided and started out. Again they sang. They stopped very briefly between hymns and continued in full voice.

They came to another field and went straight to the stream they had reckoned on.

It was dry.

They had tramped about four miles away from their meeting point, and they were growing humourless and irritable.

All that changed to anxiety and fear when they found that the third stream was also dry.

'Wha' we goin' do now?' Beneba asked.

1 This passage comes from the middle of a story. This makes it more difficult for you to work out exactly what is happening. What questions do you need to ask to understand better what is going on? Write them down.
2 Have a guess at the answers to the questions you have asked. Write your answers down.

3　Write down all the *facts* you can work out from the passage about
　these topics:
　　The place
　　The time
　　The characters
　　What they are doing
4　The passage ends with Beneba asking a question. How do you
　think the others answer it?

Section B　Stalemate

☐ Read the passage through and then answer the questions that follow
it.

'Keep lookin' some more,' Miriam said.
'Look where, though?' Quasheba asked.
"Cross anodder field,' Juba said feebly.
'Might as well,' Miriam said, wiping her face with her apron and
sighing wearily.

And off they went again, singing half-heartedly and stumbling
along, nearly falling from fatigue and despondency.

Their fear became greater when they saw to their horror that the
fourth stream was stone-dry. They didn't know where to go from
there, so they sat down beside the dry bed and rested for a while.

The day was coming noisily alive with a criss-cross of bird-song
and croaks and clicking sounds from field insects. It was a confusing
melody that had its own individual appeal. It could just as easily
enchant or annoy.

Miriam and her friends hardly noticed it. When they did, it tended
to annoy them, if only because it reminded them that the time was
passing rapidly and the morning was slipping away fast and nothing
had been achieved.

Quasheba had her head in her hands, with her fingers beating a
tattoo on her temples. She was imagining what her husband, Cubbe-
nah, would say if she came home empty-handed. She knew he would
understand. But he would become even more worried than he
already was about the drought. Miss Carpenter had at least held out
some sort of hope by saying that everybody should lay in an ample
store of water. No water, no hope. And there Quasheba's thoughts
ran into a blind alley.

Beneba, too, was worried about Quashie and their son Jeremiah.
Cudjoe and Simeon were also in Juba's thoughts.
Miriam was thinking seriously of giving up entirely and going

back home to Jacob and asking him to help plan another early morning search in which he and the other men would join; but she wondered about her chances if she continued on her present trek with Quasheba, Beneba and Juba. Would the stream they came to next be the one they were hoping for? And if it were, would the water be clean and deep enough to fill all the containers they had brought along? She remembered the first stream. It had a good depth of water and the banks were far apart. Maybe it would be best to go back to it and make the best of it, muddy and litter-strewn as it was. Naturally, the water would have to be very carefully collected, slowly and expertly, and later on, strained, boiled and strained over and over again. Would the others agree to return?

They were all tired, defeated and out of sorts. Their limbs ached with the aimless wandering and with the crossing and recrossing of the rugged hilly fields.

Miriam looked at her friends and tried to time her request for the best possible moment. She heard their restless breathing and their quiet, stifled sighs of distress.

The sounds of the morning circled everything, hovering over the women and penetrating their innermost thoughts, their half-hopes and their doubts.

Miriam looked around her and took in all the peaceful scurrying of the wild bees, the grasshoppers, the beetles and the other tiny creatures inching their way in a ragged procession along the low bank of the dry bed of the stream.

Quasheba got up and stretched. The other two women yawned.

This was Miriam's cue to make her request.

1 Write down the names of the four women. Against each one write that woman's husband and the names of any other members of her family who are mentioned.
   Example   **Beneba**   *husband – Quashie*
   son – Jeremiah

2 Who do you think Miss Carpenter is and what is her part in the story?
3 What were the arguments *for* and *against* going back to the first stream?
4 How do you think the women react to Miriam's request?

Section C   Water

☐ Read the passage through and then answer the questions that follow it.

The sun was now beating down fiercely on the field, hammering away intensely like a monotonous session of revivalist drums.

The perspiration marks on the backs of the women's long dresses were large, abstract and ugly. Their skin showed through in odd spots, as it clung to their thin calico blouses. They were all beginning to feel the burden of the heat and the hopelessness of the journey.

Miriam stood and said to no one in particular, 'The firs' stream had water.'

Quasheba frowned.

Beneba placed her arms akimbo.

Juba laughed a 'bad' laugh.

Miriam knew that her idea was going to be opposed. Yet she had nothing to lose by proposing it.

'We could go back an' see if we can get anyt'ing from it if we do it cautious like,' she said, still not talking to anyone directly.

The others started moving about and really doing nothing special.

'Soon be twelve o'clock hot sun before we can 'quint,' she continued. 'We better turn back an' collec' from the firs' stream. The strainin' an' boilin' will make it clean enough to drink an' cook with when the dry time take set.'

Quasheba shook her head defiantly.

So did Beneba.

Juba touched Miriam's shoulder.

'Wha' the use, Mirie?' she said sympathetically. 'Wha' the use?'

Miriam, however, was not easily put off. The apparent indifference of her friends to her suggestion wasn't going to stop her from trying to lessen their depression. She realized that, as Jacob's wife, she was, more or less, expected to assume the responsibility of leadership and protectiveness among her women friends when the occasion arose. She hoped that they would allow her to do so now that such a situation had arisen. She picked up her kerosene tin and bucket and waited to see what they were going to do.

Quasheba and Beneba held the handles of their hand-carts. Juba reached out for her two demi-johns.

Then it suddenly occurred to Miriam that she had foolishly ruled out the possibility that they might want to go on instead of returning to the first stream.

Nain people were a house-proud, hopeful people. Hoping was their community prayer. It had to be, living on the land as they did and always finding themselves pitted against violent storms and a host of agricultural hazards and confused by the restrictions and promises of the Parish Council.

Even the way they kept their water supply going was enough to point to their incredible optimistic nature. The asphalt drums in their kitchens and their outside storage units were filled by downpours of rain and by regular visits to the various streams in the area.

Miriam walked up to the first steep rise, at the edge of the field from which they had just climbed down, and leant against it and said, 'We could keep walkin' on if you all want to.'

Juba winked her approval. She had expected Miriam to find a way out.

'We can do that, yes,' Quasheba said.

'I don't mind,' Beneba said, 'but it's so late already that we won't be able to make more than one trip if we find water.'

'There's always tomorrow,' Juba said.

'Or we can come back later today,' Miriam said, 'after we pack the children off to school.'

They all agreed that they should go on and they started crossing the field. And they sang the loudest they had for the morning.

Their fifth attempt was fortunately their last; they found a broad, deep stream in the shady corner of a sun-baked field two miles away from the one they had left behind.

They dropped everything they were carrying, ran towards it, and threw themselves down by the water's edge. They laughed and scooped up the clean, tepid water. And drank it gratefully.

1   How did Miriam know that her idea was going to be opposed?
2   What arguments did she use to try to persuade the other women?
3   Explain in your own words *exactly* what it was that 'suddenly occurred to Miriam'.
4   Why do you think that when the women set off again they 'sang the loudest they had for the morning'?
5   How did the women feel when they found water? How do you know?

Section D   Writing

Write one of the following conversations:
a)   Miriam tells her husband about the search for water.
b)   Beneba tells Jeremiah about the search.
c)   On the way back Quasheba and Juba talk about finding water and about their opinions of Miriam.

17 BREAD

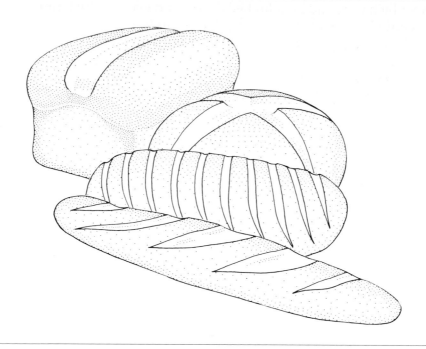

Section A   What bread is made of

Six sentences have been missed out from the passage that follows. They are listed – in the wrong order – at the end.

☐ Read the passage and work out which sentence should go in which space.

☐ Write the number of each space and against it write the letter of the sentence you have chosen.

There are many, many different kinds of bread, but the ones we know best are made from wheat flour. Usually the flour is white because all of the outside coatings of each grain are removed when the wheat is ground. What is left has been bleached to make it even whiter. Sometimes part of the bran or outside coating is left in the flour instead of being sifted out.————————1————————

Not all bread made with white wheat flour is the same. Sometimes the bread is flat and hard or tough. But the bread that most people in this country buy in a food store in sliced loaves is high and light and soft, full of millions of air holes. It is that way because it has been made with yeast.

When yeast is combined with dough made with flour and left in a warm place, a strange thing happens. The ball of dough begins to grow until it is twice its original size. —————————2— ————————————— But chemists can explain it very simply.

Yeast is a tiny living plant that floats in the air like a speck of dust. When enough of these almost invisible yeast plants combine with the sugar that is a natural part of flour, they ferment the dough, or make it 'sour'. —————————3————————————— The bubbles are trapped because wheat flour has in it something called gluten that causes the dough to stretch instead of break when the bubbles expand. The bubbles cannot escape, and as more and more of them are formed, the ball of dough gets bigger and bigger, or rises. Kneading the dough makes sure the bubble-forming gas is evenly spread through the dough. When the bread is baked, the gas disappears, but the shape of the bubbles stays in the bread.

Most people think bread tastes best when it is light and airy. —————————4————————————— In some places in the world people prefer to eat flat bread that has been made without yeast or anything else to 'leaven' it, that is, to fill it with bubbles and make it lighter.

And not everyone uses wheat flour to make bread ———————— —————5————————————— In those places rye and oats and barley are used instead of wheat for making bread. And because wheat can't grow where it is hot and wet, people in the tropics use the roots of certain plants to make their bread. These grains and roots do not have enough gluten to make stretchy dough, so they cannot be used to make raised bread.

Many people have a special feeling about their bread, no matter how strange and unbreadlike it might seem to us. ———————— —————6————————————— Perhaps this is because bread has been the world's most important food for such a long time, since before men could write their own history. The story of bread is really the story of people, too.

a) Wheat can't grow where it is too cold and the growing season is short.
b) But not everyone does.
c) When you see it happen, it seems like a kind of magic.
d) In fermentation, carbon dioxide is formed, and the gas makes bubbles in the dough.
e) They treat it with a respect that they do not have for a bunch of carrots, for example, or a slice of meat.
f) That whole-wheat flour is dark, and the bread made from it is brown.

☐ Read the passage and then follow the instructions at the end.

A   There are three methods used by large bakeries for making bread.
    The 'straight dough' method is very much like the way bread is made at home, except that machinery is used to do most of the operations and, of course, the quantities are much larger. Every bakery has a different way of doing things, but generally a bakery that uses the straight dough method works like this:

B   The flour is brought to the bakery in huge tank trucks and is pumped directly from the truck into storage tanks inside the bakery. Some tanks hold as much as 100,000 pounds of flour, and since a bakery in full production may use that much in a single day, there are several storage tanks containing reserve supplies of flour.

C   Pumps and blowers move the flour from the storage tanks through pipes to smaller storage bins near the dough mixers, huge drums with polished metal blades like part of a giant eggbeater. This machine does the heavy work of blending and kneading the ingredients. If a dough that will weigh 1,300 pounds is being prepared, the man in charge sets the controls to measure 700 pounds of flour out of the storage bin. Yeast, dried milk, honey, salt dissolved in water, and liquid shortening – a total of about 240 pounds – are added. Then a valve is opened to admit 360 pounds of water.

D   When all of the ingredients have been measured, the mixer is turned on to run for about a quarter of an hour. Cool water circulates around the mixer to keep it from heating up and raising the temperature of the dough. After the mixing is finished, the door of the mixer is opened and the soft dough tumbles into a long metal trough (we usually pronounce that word TROFF, but bakers call it a TROW, to rhyme with dough). The troughs are covered and set aside to let the dough rise for about two hours.

E   When the dough has risen, the trough is hoisted mechanically, and the contents are dumped into the divider. This machine cuts off lumps of dough at the rate of eighty-six a minute, each exactly measured by weight. The lumps drop onto a belt that carries them into the rounder, which tosses them around a bit and forms them into balls. Each ball drops into a pan that is moved into the intermediate proofer. ('To proof' is a baker's term that means 'to let rise'.) There the dough simply rests for a few minutes at room temperature. If you were to try to knead and shape the dough as it comes out of the rounder, it would be almost too elastic to work with. But when it comes out of the intermediate proofer, it is 'relaxed' and can be handled easily.

F   The pans dump their balls of dough onto a belt that carries them into the molder, which squashes them quite flat to remove all the air bubbles, curls them into jelly-roll shapes, gives them another squeeze to compress the rolled-up dough, and drops the loaves into pans.

G   The pans of dough are then carried into the proofer, where the loaves will be allowed to rise in warm, slightly damp air for about an hour. All this time the bread is moving continually. Because more loaves are always being made, some loaves are leaving the proofer as others are entering. Sometimes the dough is allowed to rise in open pans, which produce loaves with rounded tops. Bread that is made into a square-sliced sandwich loaf is baked in pans with a lid to prevent the dough from rising above the top of the pan.

H   Then the loaves are ready for the oven. The pans move at the same steady rate through the huge ovens for about a half hour. When the baked bread emerges, it is greeted with a jet blast of cold air that loosens it from the pan. Then a depanner takes over. A little rubber suction cup lifts the loaf of hot bread out of the pan, the pan goes off in one direction to be used again, and the bread is dropped onto another belt to be carried through a cooling area for an hour and a half. When it is cool enough, it is sliced, wrapped, sealed, bagged, and boxed in cartons for shipment, all by machine.

I   The whole process has taken about five hours, from the time the ingredients were fed into the mixer until the finished loaves tumbled into the shipping cartons. From the original 1,300 pounds of dough, about 1,120 one-pound loaves have been made. The difference in weight of 180 pounds is lost in the evaporation of water.

1   There are nine main paragraphs, lettered A to I. A suitable title for paragraph A might be *The 'straight dough' method*. The titles that follow could be used for paragraphs B,C,D,E – but they are printed here in the wrong order.
     1   Proofing
     2   Measuring the ingredients
     3   Mixing and rising
     4   The flour
    Work out which title belongs to which paragraph.
2   Make up titles for the remaining four paragraphs.
3   The passage lists a number of main stages in the making of bread. List them and give each one a number. Warning: some paragraphs describe more than one stage.
4   'The whole process has taken about five hours.' Work out how those five hours are used, and then write down what you have worked out.

Section C   A recipe

☐ Read the passage and then follow the instructions *after* it.

The most important element in baking bread is temperature. Remember that yeast is a living thing, a tiny plant, and you must take care of it. If the liquid you mix with it is too cold, nothing will happen – just as a plant will not grow in cold weather. If it is too hot, the yeast will die, like a plant that has been scorched by the sun. Yeast grows best at a temperature close to the temperature of your body. So the water or milk you mix with it should feel warm on your hand, but not hot. And anything else that you add, like eggs, should not be used cold from the refrigerator. If you forget to take them out ahead of time, just put them in a bowl of warm water (not hot – you don't want to cook them) for a few minutes.

There are many recipes for making all kinds of bread – white bread, dark bread, fancy holiday bread from other countries – but here is a good simple recipe to begin with. It will take about two hours from the time you start until the buns are ready to eat.

Fun Buns
You will need two mixing bowls – one large, one small – measuring cup and spoons, a table knife for making the measurements level, a spoon for mixing, two cookie sheets,* and:

1 cup hot water	*1 package dry yeast*
¼ cup vegetable oil	*1 egg*
2 tablespoons sugar	*3½ cups flour (approximately)*
1½ teaspoons salt	

Put the hot water in the small mixing bowl and add the oil, sugar, and salt. Stir the mixture well. Test the water mixture with your finger. If it feels warm but not hot, it is ready. If it is too hot, wait a few minutes and test it again.

Put the yeast and one cup of flour in the big mixing bowl. Stir them with the spoon. Pour in the warm water mixture and stir it to make a smooth batter.

Add the egg and one more cup of flour. Stir again until smooth.

Add the third cup of flour. Mix with the spoon and with your hands. Don't worry about getting messy hands. Mix it with your hands until it stops sticking to the sides of the bowl. Add a little more flour if it keeps sticking.

Sprinkle some flour on the table where you are working. Dust some on your hands. Pour the soft dough out on the floury table.

*baking trays

This is how to knead the dough: Fold the blob of dough in half as well as you can and press down on it hard with the 'heels' of both hands to flatten it. Turn the flattened dough about a quarter of the way around. Fold it in half and press down again. Dust more flour on your hands if they are sticky. Turn-fold-press, turn-fold-press, about fifteen times. By then the dough should be elastic and not at all sticky.

Cut the blob of kneaded dough in half with a knife. Cut each half in three parts. Cut each part in half again. Pat each of the twelve pieces into the shape of a hamburger bun.

Grease the two cookie sheets well with butter or margarine. Put six buns on each sheet with plenty of space between each bun. Cover the buns lightly with a piece of plastic wrap. Put the buns in a warm place – near a radiator, for instance, or in a warm closet,* but not on top of the stove with the burners on. Let them rise for about an hour or until the balls of dough are twice as big as they were.

Fifteen minutes before the hour is up, turn on the oven (or have someone help you do it) and let it heat to 375°. Put one cookie sheet on each oven shelf. Bake the buns for fifteen minutes, until they are golden brown. Check to make sure the buns on the higher shelf are not browning too fast. If they seem to be, exchange the two sheets of buns: move the bottom pan to the upper shelf and the top pan to the lower shelf. Bake five minutes more. Take them out of the oven and let them cool a little.

You can serve Fun Buns whole as dinner rolls or slice them in half to make hamburger buns or any kind of sandwich.

A recipe that is written out in paragraphs is sometimes difficult to follow. Most recipes can be divided into a number of *main stages*. Within each main stage there are a number of *separate things to do*. This recipe could be divided into four main stages. Number 3 might be titled *Letting the dough rise*, while number 4 might be *Baking*.
1   What would you call stage 1 and stage 2?
2   Stage 1 is the most complicated. How many different *things to do* does it list? Write them down.
3   Make a list of the separate things to do in stages 2, 3 and 4.

Section D   Writing

Imagine that your class has been taken on a visit to a large bakery. Write a description of what you saw and were told.

*cupboard

18 MILITARY TRAINING

Section A   Listen to the sergeant

☐ Read the passage and then answer the questions that follow it.

Stand at . . . ease!
    Sta-and . . . easy!
    Chew nut if you want, lads.
    Right, what we're going on with this morning is Use of the Shield against the Sling. This ain't a tactic as you'll find yourselves having to use often, but you've got to know about it, case you ever find yourselves drafted for a punitive raid into sheep country.
    Did I hear someone say *What's so bad about sheep?* Nothing, lad, till you want to nobble a flock for booty and they don't fancy going the way you're going. But it's not sheep you've got to watch out for, it's shepherds! Fellers from rough hill country, what've been driving off

foxes and jackals – bears, even – from their flocks all their lives. Shepherd loses an animal and he'll have to pay his master for it, unless he can show him the carcase of the animal that took it. Right?

Now, see where the banner's set up outside the Captain's tent? How many javelin throws would you reckon to reach that in?

Two! Don't be stupid! That's three and a quarter throws by a javelineer, first-class! None of you lot'd reach it in five, except perhaps Lefty there. Now, suppose you was standing in javelin-throw of that there banner, aiming at the pole, how often would you hit it in five shots? Not once, none of you – and that includes you, Lefty, so stop grinning. But a shepherd what's handy with his sling would hit that pole five times out of five, close range. From here . . . oh, twice out of five, maybe.

So that's the first thing you've got to get into your heads. A sling's got five times the range what a javelin has, and getting on five times the accuracy. What it's *not* got is the weight, and that's what gives you your chance against a slinger.

Provided. You. Know. How. To. Use. Your. Shield!

Right. Now I'm going to tell you a story as isn't in the manual, but it's as good an illustration as you could ask for how *not* to tackle a slinger. Eight years back I was on prisoner-escort, marching home from taking Jerusalem. I got talking with one of them Hebrews – we'd had one hell of a siege, starving them out – and he was trying to tell me that starving as they were we'd still not have taken Jerusalem if they'd had a couple of hundred fellers like David on the walls.

David? I say. Who's David? This is what he tells me.

1 Explain in a few sentences what is going on here.
2 This is the beginning of a well known story told in an unusual way. What is the story?

Section B Preparations for battle

☐ Read the passage and then answer the questions that follow it.

Long time back the Hebrews were nothing but a pack of wild tribes in the hills. Then they started having trouble with their neighbours, a lot called Philistines, lived down on the coast, a notch or two more civilized than the Hebrews by the sound of it. Trying to get a bit of discipline into the tribes, the Hebrews chose themselves a King, big feller called Saul, and he put an army of a sort together and caught the Philistines two or three times unexpected. Naturally the Philistines wanted to put a stop to that, so they sent a real army up into the hills, teach the Hebrews a lesson, show them who's master. They didn't just go burning and looting, the usual way – they made a real propaganda effort. They'd got hold of a professional soldier, a giant of a man, nine feet tall my Hebrew said. His armour weighed as much as what I do, and you'd have had a job even to lift his javelin. Ruddy great shield, too, big as a door.

The Philistines manoeuvred around till they'd got the terrain they wanted for the exercise, a shallow valley with the armies drawn up on opposite slopes and a nice big space in the middle, so everybody had a good view. Then they sent the giant out in front of the battle-line, with his shield-bearer toddling beside him, and the giant strode up and down yelling at the Hebrews to send a man out to fight him. Just as you'd expect, nobody durst, and things were looking bad for King Saul. You see, a wild army like that, first and foremost it's a question of morale. They can do anything provided they're winning – I've seen a tribal charge get in among seasoned troops and wipe them clean off the battlefield – but as soon as they're losing they're no use at all. They just melt away. So that was the Philistine tactic – keep the giant parading up and down challenging them to come and fight till they start slipping back to their farms and then where's King Saul's army?

So Saul was at his wit's end when who says he'll take the giant on, but his own minstrel, lad called David? That's another thing about shepherds – sitting out alone on the hills all day they get handy with little home-made harps, or reed pipes, or some such. Keep themselves happy. This David had been doing a bit of that, or rather keeping the King happy when he was down, but now he said he'd take the giant on.

King Saul was so desperate he'd try anything. He wanted David to wear the King's own armour, look a bit impressive in front of the troops, at least, but that wasn't David's idea. Next morning David took his sling and went and chose himself a few pebbles out of a dry river bed, a bit heavier than what he'd use for jackals and such. He wasn't going to need the range, see? It was the weight what mattered. I dare say he took a couple of practice shots. I would.

1   Make a list of the main events that this passage describes. Number them and put them in order, starting like this:

> 1. The Hebrews form an army.
> 2. They make Saul their leader.
> 3. . . . . . .

2   Who was the giant?
3   Why was he sent to parade up and down in front of the Hebrews?
4   What preparations did David make to face the challenge?

Section C Mistakes

☐ Read the passage through and then answer the questions that follow.

Now, I want you to imagine you're this giant, parading up and down in front of the battle line, yelling at the savages to send somebody out to fight you. Last three days nobody's come and it's getting a bit monotonous. Then, all of a sudden there's this little feller coming towards you, not a sign of a weapon on him, not a scrap of armour. Right shoulder bare.

Mistake number one. You don't recognize him for a slinger. Bare right shoulder – that's the giveaway.

You can't believe he's serious so you shout to scare him off. He shouts back and comes on, so you go and meet him.

Mistake number two. You make yourself a target. Against slingers the rule is Stay In Rank. Move forward, yes, on command – shorten the range till you can get the javelins going. But . . . Stay. In. Rank!

You're still this giant, remember, and perhaps you're not so thick you don't guess the little feller's going to try and chuck something at you, so you take your shield from your shield-bearer, who's glad to get rid of it.

Mistake number three. Wrong sort of shield. Big as a door, didn't I tell you? Now this here's the right sort of shield – Babylonian Standard Issue – just the job against slingers, big enough to cover the head and neck, light enough to whip into place and out. Point is, a slinger always aims at the head. Slingshot's never got the weight to get through armour. Right? So all you've got to guard is the head.

Now mistake number four comes back to mistake number one, and what was that? Recognize your enemy, wasn't it? Know what he's likely to get up to. But you're this giant, blundering forward wearing armour as heavy as a man, with your great clumsy shield on your arm and your great clumsy spear in your hand. Are you watching what the little feller's up to? No, you're not. All you're thinking of is getting close and smashing him to jelly. He's running towards you, but all of a sudden he stops and strikes a pose . . . so! Look at me, lads! Legs well apart, see? Torso swung round so his left shoulder's pointing dead at you . . . so! That's how you can tell it's *you* he's aiming at, and not some feller five along in the rank. His right arm goes back. You can see that little jiggle of his wrist where the sling's spinning round. You won't see the sling – it's moving too fast. Now his right arm whips over . . . so!

Up with your shield! Clang!

Backward angle on the shield, see, glance the shot upward, not down onto your feet or sideways into your next-door's face. Then, soon as you hear that lovely clang, down shield so you can watch what the beggar's doing next. Easy as husking lentils when you've got the hang of it.

But did our giant know any of this? Did he hell. There he was, barging forward, shield down, bellowing his challenges, when David's first stone caught him slap in the middle of his great thick forehead. Not thick enough poor feller. Down he went like a tower falling in a siege and David ran up and whipped the giant's own sword out and hacked his head off.

Mind you, it wasn't only the death of the giant. Look what happened to the propaganda drive. The Philistines see their champ in all his armour carved up by a little Hebrew without any weapons at all – and the Hebrews see it too. Before the Philistines have got over the shock the tribesmen are coming at them in a whirling mob. No time to form rank, go into defensive drill, because now the tribesmen are in among them . . . and that was one punitive strike what got punished and struck.

Right! Spit your nut out! Ten-shun! Shield-drill, anti-sling, by numbers! On the command *One!* . . .

1 What were the four mistakes the giant made?
2 Explain in your own words what the sergeant says the men should do to defend themselves against a slinger. Put the actions in order and number them. Start like this:

> 1. Use the right shield.
> 2. Watch the enemy.
> 3. . . . . . .

3 What was the result of the death of the giant?

Section D   Writing

Tell the story as if you were one of the people involved. You can be David, Saul or a member of either army.

19 THE MOONPATH

Section A The dancing bear

Section A introduces the *place* where this story happens and the main *characters* who take part in it. This introduction has to give the reader a lot of information and ideas. As he reads, the reader asks himself questions about the place and the characters – or he should. As he reads further into the story he begins to find out the answers to these questions.

☐ At each point marked *, stop reading. Ask yourself at least one question about what you have just read. Write your questions down. At the end of the section see how many of them have been answered. When you have finished the whole story look again to see how many of them have been answered.

97

If the world were flat, and if you could look straight into the rising sun, you would see the land where Nick and Bruin lived. It was a land of sticky days and breathless nights, where the sun came up like an enemy and the wind had flies in it.

At the edge of this land, where bitter waves met hot sand, there lay a town of flat, ugly buildings and narrow streets and in one of these streets stood a blacksmith's forge.*

Nick was apprenticed to the blacksmith. All day in his stiff leather apron he worked by the stinging-hot furnace; pumping the bellows or carrying bars of iron for his master. At night he lay on the dusty floor with a chain on his foot. Nick's mother and father had sold him to the blacksmith for seven years. Nick cried for them sometimes, in the night, but he hated them too, and vowed they would never see him again.*

Sometimes Nick's master loaded the things he had made on to a handcart, and Nick pulled it through the town to the customers' homes. As he went along, Nick would search the faces of the people he passed. He always hoped for a smile, or a kindly word, but he never found one. It was a mean, ugly town full of mean, ugly people.*

One afternoon as he was hauling the cart across town he saw that a small crowd had gathered in the square. There were shouts, and some laughter. Nick left the cart and went over to look. He was small and thin, and easily slipped through to the front. In the middle of the crowd, on a small patch of beaten dust, stood a bear. There was a collar round its neck with a chain. A man held the chain in one hand and a stick in the other. As Nick watched, the man poked the bear with the stick and cried, 'Down, Bruin!' The bear's legs collapsed and it rolled over in the dust and lay still, playing dead. The people laughed. Somebody dropped a coin in the man's hat. 'Up, Bruin!' cried the man, and he jerked on the chain. The bear clambered slowly to its feet. Nick wondered what it felt like to have a coat of thick fur on such a day as this.*

The man jabbed his stick into the bear's side. 'Dance, Bruin!' he snarled.

The bear lifted its forepaws and began a slow shuffle on its hind feet, swinging its great head from side to side.

'Faster!' cried the man, and he struck the creature across its paws.*

The people laughed. Bruin tried to move a little faster. There was a cloud of flies round its head; they settled near its eyes.

The man put down the stick and produced a battered mouth-organ. He sucked and blew a scratchy tune, and a few more coins fell into the hat. Bruin moved heavily to the thin music. After a while the man stopped playing and the bear dropped on to all four feet. People clapped a little. The man bowed and grinned.

Nick was turning sadly away when the bear raised its head and looked at him. The boy paused, gazing back into those tiny, pain-filled eyes.* In that instant, Nick felt something that made his own eyes brim, and caused him to clamp his teeth into his bottom lip. He turned and began to push his way through the crowd. He felt the bear's eyes following him and could scarcely see through the tears in his own. He lifted the handles of his cart and went on without looking back.*

Section B The fisherman's tale

☐ Read this passage carefully and then answer the question that follows it.

That night, lying on the dusty floor with the chain on his foot, Nick thought about Bruin. He saw the fly-tortured eyes and the dry, lolling tongue and he murmured softly into the dark, 'Some day, Bruin, we will leave this place, you and I. We will sail away to a land that is white and cold as the moon. There will be no flies there, and no chains.' He moved a little and his chain made a clinking sound. He sighed, and closed his eyes. 'One day,' he murmured, and then he slept, while the cold white moon slid silent down the sky.

The next morning his master said, 'Take this boat-hook to Caspar, the fisherman. You will find him on the sand, mending his nets.'

When he stepped out of the forge the sun hit him and he screwed up his eyes. 'This land is an anvil,' he told himself. 'The sun is a great hammer, and it will beat me on the anvil until I am bent and blackened like the end of this boat-hook.' He wiped the sweat from his forehead and turned towards the sea.

Caspar was sitting cross-legged in the sand, mending a net. He looked up, squinting into the sun. 'Ah, my new boat-hook is ready, yes? Give it here.'

Nick handed it to him and stood wiggling his toes in the hot sand.

The fisherman examined the boat-hook and said. 'Tell your master I am satisfied and will pay him tomorrow.'

Nick bobbed his head, and was turning away when the man said, 'I saw you, yesterday. Watching the bear.'

Nick turned. Pale blue eyes regarding him, a twinkle in them somewhere. He nodded. 'Yes. We are both slaves, the bear and I.'

He knew he ought not to have said it. Suppose the man told his master? His eyes, fearful, met Caspar's. The twinkle remained. 'Have no fear,' said the fisherman, softly. 'I have no master, but if I had, it would have been the moonpath for me, long ago.'

Nick did not understand. 'The – moonpath?' he whispered.

Caspar nodded.

'What is the moonpath?' asked Nick. Perhaps this man was mocking him.

The fisherman raised his eyebrows. 'The moonpath? Why, the moonpath is the road to freedom; a silver track that lies upon the sea.'

Nick turned, to see warm, brown water moving slug-like in the sun. His lip twisted up. 'I see no silver track,' he said.

Caspar grinned, shaking his head. 'It is not there now, little slave,' he said. His face became grave and he patted the sand beside him. 'Come, sit here and I will tell you.'

Nick approached the man, half-fearful, and sat down. Caspar set aside his net, drew up his knees under his chin, and wrapped his thick arms around them. He gazed out over the sea.

'It is big, the sea,' he said. 'It is the biggest thing on earth, and the fiercest. To cross it you need a good boat.' He glanced sidelong at Nick. 'Slaves do not have boats. But sometimes at night, in the full of the moon, there is a way for them if they believe and are brave.'

Nick waited. After a moment, Caspar nodded towards the sea. 'Out there,' he said, 'when the moon is full, there is a path across the sea. It is long and straight, and at the far end lies a land as cool as this land is hot.' He turned earnest eyes to Nick. 'He who takes the silver path must travel quickly, for it melts with the dawn and is no more until the moon is full again.'

The boy felt a lump in his throat and he gazed at Caspar through tear-filled eyes. 'I have seen such a path,' he choked. 'It is made from light. No one can walk upon it. You mock me.'

Caspar shrugged. 'I told you. A man must believe, and be brave.' He took up a net and began to work upon it as though Nick were no longer there.

After a while the boy blinked away his tears, got up, and walked towards the town.

☐ What do you think happens to Nick? What happens to the bear? What happens to the other characters? Write your own conclusion to the story.

Section C   The moonpath

☐ Read the passage and then answer the question that follows.

Many days passed. One evening, at the end of a very hard day, Nick's master beat him and left him waterless. Nick lay a long time crying in the dust. When he had cried all his tears, he sat up and rubbed his eyes with the heels of his hands so that the dust from them made a grey paste on his cheeks.

'I will not stay here,' he told himself, 'to be beaten and starved and roasted. I will run away. I will go tonight.' And he crawled across the floor to where his master had left a large file. His chain was barely long enough, but by lying at full stretch he was able to get his finger-tips to it. He laid the blade across a link and, working rapidly, began to saw at the iron.

An hour he worked, then rested, gasping. He blinked away the sweat and went on. At midnight the link parted. Nick scrambled to his feet and stood, listening. The moon-washed streets were silent.

He left the forge on tiptoe, flitting from shadow to shadow along the road. He did not know where he would go. The town was surrounded on three sides by the desert, and on the other by the sea. The desert, then. He must try to cross the desert. He turned up an alley, and cried out in terror. His master came swiftly, crouching, the great hammer drawn back over a brawny shoulder. Nick whirled and fled.

'Runaway!' roared his master behind him.

His voice echoed all across the midnight town. A door was flung open. Then another. Lights moved in windows. People spilled out of houses. Nick swerved and ran on. The people were shouting to one another. His way was blocked. He spun round. Men, strung out across the street behind him, and his master like some squat ape coming with the hammer. He ran left. A figure crouched, spreading huge arms. He spun. There! A clear run. He gasped, pelting along the unguarded alley, and as he ran he cried out, without knowing it, the name of the only other slave he knew. 'Bruin! Bruin! Bruin! . . .'

Breaking clear of the buildings he glanced over his shoulder. His master followed, closer now, his hammer raised high. Nick ran on desperately then stopped, skidding in damp sand. The sea! They had driven him to the sea! He turned, sobbing, and angled along the beach, dodging between huge rocks and leaping over small ones. He could hear the pounding of his master's boots and the rasping of his breath. He threw back his head and ran wild-eyed, mouth agape. He never saw the rock. It struck him below the knees and he went headlong in the sand. He rolled and screamed, flinging up his arms to cover his face. His master raised the great hammer. A cry. The hammer fell, kicking up sand by Nick's head, and then his master reeled, clutching his side.

A shaggy form swayed erect against the moon, snarling. Bruin! The bear turned, a short length of chain swinging at its neck. Nick gazed up at the great head and then beyond, to where the moon hung cool and full in the velvet sky. Cool and full. Caspar! The boy looked seaward, and it was there. 'I believe!' sobbed Nick.

Men were coming, running quiet in the sand. He scrambled to his feet. 'Come, Bruin!' he cried.

The sand sloped gently down, and they ran; not into surf, but on to rippled silver, cool and hard. 'I believe!' cried Nick, and they moved out across the midnight sea.

And all along the shore the people stood, their mouths open, staring. One stuck out his foot and snatched it back, drenched with moon-white spray. So they stood, all night, gazing out to sea. From time to time someone would shake his head, or mutter something under his breath. And when it was near to dawn, they looked at one another out of the corners of their eyes, and shuffled their feet, and began to drift away in ones and twos. They walked by the blacksmith, who nursed his side by a rock. And the blacksmith said to one, 'Where is my boy?', and to another, 'What happened?' But they just shook their heads like people in a dream.

And then the bear's master came dangling the broken lock from Bruin's cage. Far, far away, a cooling wind ruffled Nick's hair and Bruin dropped his head to lap the snow.

☐ The blacksmith returns to his house. The next day Nick's father is passing through the town and calls on the blacksmith. He asks where his son is. The blacksmith has to tell him what has happened. Write their conversation.

What happens next?

While we are reading stories we often have a guess about what will happen next. In this section that is what you will be asked to do. It contains five stories. Each one is divided into parts. After each part there are questions asking you to guess what you think will happen in the next part. So that people are not tempted to cheat, all the parts are jumbled up and numbered. You will be told the number of the part you have to read.

1 | Security Check   *Arthur C. Clarke*

It is often said in our age of assembly lines and mass production that there's no room for the individual craftsman, the artist in wood or metal who made so many of the treasures of the past. Like most generalizations, this simply isn't true. He's rarer now, of course, but he's certainly not extinct. He has often had to change his vocation, but in his modest way he still flourishes. Even on the island of Manhattan he may be found, if you know where to look for him. Where rents are low and fire regulations unheard of, his minute, cluttered workshops may be discovered in the basements of apartment houses or in the upper storeys of derelict shops. He may no longer make violins or cuckoo clocks or music boxes, but the skills he uses are the same as they always were, and no two objects he creates are ever identical. He is not contemptuous of mechanization: you will find several electric hand tools under the debris on his bench. He has moved with the times: he will always be around, the universal odd-job man who is never aware of it when he makes an immortal work of art.

Hans Muller's workshop consisted of a large room at the back of a deserted warehouse, no more than a vigorous stone's throw from the Queensborough Bridge. Most of the building had been boarded up awaiting demolition, and sooner or later Hans would have to move. The only entrance was across a weed-covered yard used as a parking place during the day, and much frequented by the local juvenile delinquents at night. They had never given Hans any trouble, for he knew better than to co-operate with the police when they made their periodic enquiries. The police fully appreciated his delicate position and did not press matters, so Hans was on good terms with everybody. Being a peaceable citizen, that suited him very well.

The work that Hans was now engaged on would have deeply puzzled his Bavarian ancestors. Indeed, ten years ago it would have puzzled Hans himself. And it had all started because a bankrupt client had given him a TV set in payment for services rendered . . .

Hans had accepted the offer reluctantly, not because he was old-fashioned and disapproved of TV, but simply because he couldn't imagine where he could find time to look at the darned thing. Still, he thought, at least I can always sell it for fifty dollars. But before I do that, let's see what the programmes are like . . .

a) *What are your first impressions of Hans?*
b) *What do you think happened when he did sample TV programmes – and why?*

2 | A Good Six Penn'orth   *Bill Naughton*

The ground under our feet was slushy, and the glaring lights illuminated an almost deserted Fair. We liked it that way. Our heads stopped reeling, and we were able to stroll about the place and savour the atmosphere without being overcome and spending our money rashly.

'Take it easy,' I warned my mates, 'and let's keep scouting round till we've found the top value for money.'

We watched the Flying Pigs, Big Boats, Bumper Cars, all going cheap, but we clung to our sixpences. We inspected every game of chance and skill: Hoopla, All Press, Dartboards, Ringboards, Roll-a-Penny, Skittles, Bagatelle, Rifle Range, and Coconut Shies.

'Look at that hairy 'un,' whispered Harry. 'I've allus wanted to knock off a coconut – and I reckon that 'ud drop with a touch.'

'That's what you think,' I said.

'I vote we have a good feed of them hot peas,' said Basher. 'Just smell 'um. What you spend on your guts, my Mum reckons, is never lost.'

'Don't rush it, Basher,' I said.

'A coconut's the best bet,' said Harry. 'You might even knock *two* off – and they'd last for days.'

'We didn't come by our money so easy,' I cautioned them, 'so let's use our discretion afore we part with it.'

At that moment my eye caught sight of the figure of a man in silk shirt and riding-breeches, a silver-handled whip in his hand, poised on a platform beneath the brightest lights on the fairground.

'Ladies and gentlemen,' called out a beautiful blonde lady. 'Introducing Waldo – the greatest lion-tamer of all time. Any moment now he will enter the cage of Nero! Nero the Untamable! The African jungle lion that has killed four trainers – the largest lion in Europe – the fiercest in captivity. Waldo will positively enter his cage! Will he come out alive?'

a) *What do you think the storyteller wanted to spend his money on?*
b) *Why?*

3 The Wheelbarrow Boy   *Richard Parker*

'Now see here, Thomis,' I said, 'I've just about had enough of you. If you haven't settled yourself down and started some work in two minutes' time I shall turn you into a wheelbarrow. I'm not warning you again.'

Of course, Thomis was not the only one: the whole class had the fidgets: he just happened to be the one I picked on. It was a windy day, and wind always upsets kids and makes them harder to handle. Also, I happened to know that Thomis's father had won a bit of money on the Pools, so it was easy to understand the boy's being off balance. But it's fatal to start making allowances for bad behaviour.

After about three minutes I called out, 'Well, Thomis? How many sums have you done?'

'I'm just writing the date,' said the boy sullenly.

'Right,' I said. 'You can't say I didn't warn you.'

What happened next?

4 Friedrich   *Hans Peter Richter*

In Germany in the 1930s the Nazi party, led by Hitler, stirred up hatred against the Jews. There were many laws which made life very difficult for the Jews. In addition, gangs of people went round smashing Jewish property and attacking Jewish families. In this story the narrator is a schoolboy who is friendly with the Jewish boy next door, Friedrich Schneider. One day the narrator is walking home from school and sees that attacks have been made on a number of Jewish houses.

At the next corner I ran into a troop of five men and three women. They were armed with crowbars, wore helmets and headscarves. Silently they were heading for a Jewish home for apprentices.

Many curious hangers-on were following them.

'About time, too, that they get what's coming to them,' commented a little man with glasses. 'They've had it coming to them for a long time. I just hope they don't miss anyone!'

I, too, joined the group.

'Today you'll see something, boy,' the little man promised, 'that you can tell your grandchildren about.'

The group halted outside the Jewish home for apprentices. At first, they all just seemed to stand around. Then they began to mutter and exchange advice, apparently trying to give each other courage. At last, one of the men walked forward.

'Open up!' he shouted to the upper floors of the home.

But nothing stirred, no window opened, not even a curtain moved. The house seemed dead.

The man bawled his order a second time to shut windows.

Our eyes were all glued to the building. I was very excited. What would happen?

Nothing did!

One of the women reviled the Jewish home in an ugly voice.

I couldn't understand what she said because her voice was so shrill.

The man paid no attention to the screeching. With heavy steps he marched towards the heavy oak door. He pressed down the handle, but the door was locked.

He stepped back three, four steps, and threw his back against the door. He tried again, this time taking a longer run.

Again nothing!

a) *Why did the boy join the group?*
b) *Why was he excited?*
c) *What did the people do next?*

Charles   *Shirley Jackson*

The day Laurie started kindergarten he renounced corduroy overalls with bibs and began wearing blue jeans with a belt; I watched him go off the first morning with the older girl next door, seeing clearly that an era of my life was ended, my sweet-voiced nursery-school tot replaced by a long-trousered, swaggering character who forgot to stop at the corner and wave goodbye to me.

He came home the same way, the front door slamming open, his cap on the floor, and the voice suddenly became raucous shouting, 'Isn't anybody *here*?'

At lunch he spoke insolently to his father, spilled Jannie's milk, and remarked that his teacher said that we were not to take the name of the Lord in vain.

'How *was* school today?' I asked, elaborately casual.

'All right,' he said.

'Did you learn anything?' his father asked.

Laurie regarded his father coldly. 'I didn't learn nothing,' he said.

'Anything,' I said. 'Didn't learn anything.'

'The teacher spanked a boy, though,' Laurie said, addressing his bread and butter. 'For being fresh,' he added with his mouth full.

'What did he do?' I asked. 'Who was it?'

Laurie thought. 'It was Charles,' he said. 'He was fresh. The teacher spanked him and made him stand in a corner. He was awfully fresh.'

'What did he do?' I asked again, but Laurie slid off his chair, took a cookie, and left, while his father was still saying, 'See here, young man.'

The next day Laurie remarked at lunch, as soon as he sat down, 'Well, Charles was bad again today.' He grinned enormously and said, 'Today Charles hit the teacher.'

'Good heavens,' I said, mindful of the Lord's name, 'I suppose he got spanked again?'

'He sure did,' Laurie said. 'Look up,' he said to his father.

'What?' his father said, looking up.

'Look down,' Laurie said. 'Look at my thumb. Gee, you're dumb.' He began to laugh insanely.

'Why did Charles hit the teacher?' I asked quickly.

'Because she tried to make him colour with red crayons,' Laurie said. 'Charles wanted to colour with green crayons so he hit the teacher and she spanked him and said nobody play with Charles but everybody did.'

The third day – it was Wednesday of the first week – Charles bounced a seesaw onto the head of a little girl and made her bleed and the teacher made him stay inside all during recess. Thursday Charles had to stand in a corner during storytime because he kept pounding his feet on the floor. Friday Charles was deprived of blackboard privileges because he threw chalk.

a) *What did Laurie's parents think of his first week at the kindergarten?*
b) *What do you think happened during the second week?*

6 I jumped. The glass had belonged to a bookcase. But almost at once my curiosity awoke. Gently I tapped a cracked pane of glass and it fell out of its frame. By now I was enjoying myself. I swung so hard against the third pane that its splinters fell in bursts to the floor.

With my hammer I cut myself a path through the corridors, smashing aside whatever barred my way: legs of chairs, toppled wardrobes, chamber pots and glassware. I felt so strong! I could have sung I was so drunk with the desire to swing my hammer.

I discovered a door leading to a small classroom that hadn't been touched yet. Curiously, I looked around.

Turning, I hit against a T-square with my schoolbag. It clattered to the floor and I stepped on it by mistake. It burst with a loud bang that sounded like a shot.

I stopped short. Lots more T-squares hung on the wall. I took down another and repeated the bang. This time, the sound was deeper. One after the other, I bent T-squares till they broke. And I enjoyed the fact that each had a different tone to it.

When I couldn't find any more T-squares, I picked up my hammer from the podium. I drummed it along the desk tops and searched all the cupboards and desk drawers in the room. But I found nothing else to satisfy my lust for destruction.

Disappointed, I was about to leave the room, but by the door I looked back one last time. Against the far wall stood a large blackboard. I pulled back my arm and hurled the hammer. It struck the centre of the blackboard. The head remained stuck. The light handle projected from the black surface. All of a sudden I felt tired and disgusted. On the stairs, I found half a mirror. I looked in it. Then I ran home.

a) *How did he feel as he broke things?*
b) *How did his mood change?*
c) *What did he do and say when he got home?*

7   Slowly he turned from the workbench and faced the door. It had been locked – how could it have been opened so silently? There were two men standing beside it, motionless, watching him. Hans felt his heart trying to climb into his gullet, and summoned up what courage he could to challenge them. At least, he felt thankful, he had little money here. Then he wondered if, after all, this was a good thing. They might be annoyed . . .

'Who are you?' he asked. 'What are you doing here?'

One of the men moved towards him while the other remained watching alertly from the door. They were both wearing very new overcoats, with hats low down on their heads so that Hans could not see their faces. They were too well dressed, he decided, to be ordinary hold-up men.

'There's no need to be alarmed, Mr Muller,' replied the nearer man, reading his thoughts without difficulty. 'This isn't a hold-up. It's official. We're from – Security.'

'I don't understand.'

The other reached into a portfolio he had been carrying beneath his coat, and pulled out a sheaf of photographs. He riffled through them until he had found the one he wanted.

'You've given us quite a headache, Mr Muller. It's taken us two weeks to find you – your employers were so secretive. No doubt they were anxious to hide you from their rivals. However, here we are and I'd like you to answer some questions.'

'I'm not a spy!' answered Hans indignantly as the meaning of the words penetrated. 'You can't do this! I'm a loyal American citizen!'

The other ignored the outburst. He handed over the photograph.

'Do you recognize this?' he said.

'Yes. It's the inside of Captain Zipp's spaceship.'

'And you designed it?'

'Yes.'

Another photograph came out of the file.

'And what about this?'

'That's the Martian city of Paldar, as seen from the air.'

'Your own idea?'

'Certainly,' Hans replied, now too indignant to be cautious.

'And *this*?'

'Oh, the proton gun. I was quite proud of that.'

'Tell me, Mr Muller – are these all your own ideas?'

'Yes, *I* don't steal from other people.'

His questioner turned to his companion and spoke for a few minutes in a voice too low for Hans to hear. They seemed to reach agreement on some point, and the conference was over before Hans could make his intended grab at the telephone.

a) *Who do you think the men were?*
b) *What do you think they wanted with Hans?*
c) *What do you think Hans intended to do?*

---

8 'Now look here, Teddy,' said Mr Thomis fiercely. 'Just you come to your senses this minute, or I'll bash the daylights out of you.' And as he spoke he began to unbuckle a heavy belt that was playing second fiddle to his braces.

The wheelbarrow changed back into Teddy Thomis and nipped smartly down the garden and through a hole in the fence.

'There you are,' said Mr Thomis. 'Trouble with you teachers is . . .'

Can you complete the sentence?

9 During the third and fourth weeks there seemed to be a reformation in Charles; Laurie reported grimly at lunch on Thursday of the third week, 'Charles was so good today the teacher gave him an apple.'

'What?' I said, and my husband added warily, 'You mean Charles?'

'Charles,' Laurie said. 'He gave the crayons around and he picked up the books afterward and the teacher said he was her helper.'

'What happened?' I asked incredulously.

'He was her helper, that's all,' Laurie said, and shrugged.

'Can this be true, about Charles?' I asked my husband that night. 'Can something like this happen?'

'Wait and see,' my husband said cynically. 'When you've got a Charles to deal with, this may mean he's only plotting.'

He seemed to be wrong. For over a week Charles was the teacher's helper; each day he handed things out and he picked things up; no one had to stay after school.

'The PTA meeting's next week again,' I told my husband one evening. 'I'm going to find Charles's mother there.'

'Ask her what happened to Charles,' my husband said. 'I'd like to know.'

'I'd like to know myself,' I said.

On Friday of that week things were back to normal.

a) *What was 'normal'?*
b) *What do you think happened?*

---

10 Before Basher and Harry could hold me I was at the paybox.

'Half, please.'

'*Half?* Why, you're going in for a *quarter* tonight. Two bob's the proper price. . . . You don't expect to see a chap eaten by a lion for threepence?'

I handed over the sixpence. I waved to my mates, but they wouldn't come. So I quickly went inside the tent, so as to get near the front. Inside were four people, and they looked at me pityingly. There was a well-dressed couple, an old man, and a woman who looked like a Sunday school teacher. It was very cold, and after the bright lights outside one could only see dimly. I went and stood near the stage.

There was no sign of Waldo. After a long time I heard the beating of a drum and the woman announcer. I felt like going out again and listening.

'We can't wait much longer,' I heard the man say to the woman. 'Is he never going to go in to that wretched beast?'

Only five more people came in during the next twenty minutes. I felt chilled, and I was aware of an empty spot of skin in the palm of my hand, where I had clutched the sixpence. Then there was a final beating of the drum, and Waldo appeared on the stage before me.

The next part of the story describes Waldo's act. What do you think it was like and why?

---

11   Mother was already waiting for me. She looked at me, but said nothing. I didn't tell her where I had been.

Mother served the soup. I began to eat.

At that moment, we heard yells outside our house.

The front door was pushed open, accompanied by shouts.

Herr Resch complained loudly.

Noisily many people clattered up the stairs, past our door and higher.

The Schneiders' door burst open with a bang.

'What's that?' Mother asked, pale and horrified.

We heard a cry – Frau Schneider!

'We must call the police!'

Something fell to the floor with a muffled sound.

'The police don't do anything,' I replied. 'They watch.'

A man's voice swore.

Friedrich cried out, then howled hopelessly.

I threw down my spoon and ran to the door.

'Stay here!' Mother wailed.

I raced up the stairs.

a) *Why didn't he tell his mother where he had been?*
b) *Who were the people who came to the flats?*
c) *Why did he race upstairs?*
d) *What did he see when he got there?*

12 His hand had gone out to the switch: the screen had filled with moving shapes – and, like millions of men before him, Hans was lost. He entered a world he had not known existed – a world of battling spaceships, of exotic planets and strange races – the world, in fact of Captain Zipp, Commander of the Space Legion.

Only when the tedious recital of the virtues of Crunche, the Wonder Cereal, had given way to an almost equally tedious boxing match between two muscle-bound characters who seemed to have signed a non-aggression pact, did the magic fade. Hans was a simple man. He had always been fond of fairy tales – and *this* was the modern fairy tale, with trimmings of which the Grimm Brothers had never dreamed. So Hans did not sell his TV set.

It was some weeks before the initial naive, uncritical enjoyment wore off. The first thing that began to annoy Hans was the furniture and general decor of the world of the future. He was, as has been indicated, an artist – and he refused to believe that in a hundred years taste would have deteriorated as badly as the Crunche sponsors seemed to imagine.

He also thought very little of the weapons that Captain Zipp and his opponents used. It was true that Hans did not pretend to understand the principles upon which the portable proton disintegrator was based, but however it worked, there was certainly no reason why it should be *that* clumsy. The clothes, the spaceship interiors – they just weren't convincing. How did he know? He had always possessed a highly developed sense of the fitness of things, and it could still operate even in this novel field.

We have said that Hans was a simple man. He was also a shrewd one, and he had heard that there was money in TV.

a) *Which programmes did Hans like best?*
b) *What did he dislike about them, and why?*
c) *So what do you think he did?*

13 'Oh, good,' he said. 'So the gardening requisition has started to come in at last.'

'No,' I said, dumping the barrow down in the middle of his carpet. 'This is Thomis. I told you . . .'

'Sorry,' he said. 'I'd clean forgotten. Leave him there and I'll get to work on him straight away. I'll send him back to you when he's presentable.'

I went back to my class and did a double period of composition, but no Thomis turned up. I thought the Old Man must have forgotten again, so when the bell went at twelve I took a peep into his room to jog his memory.

a) *What did he see?*
b) *Had the Headmaster been successful?*

14   At the meeting I sat restlessly, scanning each comfortable matronly face, trying to determine which one hid the secret of Charles. None of them looked to me haggard enough. No one stood up in the meeting and apologized for the way her son had been acting. No one mentioned Charles.

After the meeting I identified and sought out Laurie's kindergarten teacher. She had a plate with a cup of tea and a piece of chocolate cake; I had a plate with a cup of tea and a piece of marshmallow cake. We manoeuvred up to one another cautiously and smiled.

'I've been so anxious to meet you,' I said. 'I'm Laurie's mother.'

'We're all so interested in Laurie,' she said.

'Well, he certainly likes kindergarten,' I said. 'He talks about it all the time.'

'We had a little trouble adjusting, the first week or so,' she said primly, 'but now he's a fine little helper. With lapses, of course.'

'Laurie usually adjusts very quickly,' I said. 'I suppose this time it's Charles's influence.'

'Charles?'

'Yes,' I said, laughing, 'you must have your hands full in that kindergarten, with Charles.'

'Charles?' she said.

The teacher said one sentence and that is the end of the story. What do you think it is and why?

15 'I'm not surprised,' I said, 'the way that lion went at him. It clawed the blinking shirt off his back. He could hardly hold it at bay with his whip, an' a woman with a revolver was about to shoot it.'

'Ee, suffering Simon! An' did you see all that?'

''Course I did. Your Harry had a coconut instead.'

16 I was pulled along with the throng. When I had a chance to stop and look around me, the sounds of crashing and bumping came from all parts of the house.

As I climbed the stairs with my schoolbag, bedside tables zoomed by and burst apart at the bottom of the stairs.

All this was strangely exhilarating.

No one stopped the destruction. Of the people living in the house, none were to be seen. Nothing but empty corridors, empty rooms.

In one of the bedrooms I came across the woman who had done the shouting. She was slashing open mattresses with a vegetable knife. She smiled at me in a cloud of dust. 'Don't you know me any more?' she asked in a squeaky voice.

I thought, then shook my head.

She laughed out loud. 'When I bring you your paper every morning?' With the back of her hand, she wiped her mouth, lifted a bottle of milk to her lips and drank from it. Then she put the bottle down again and whirled the slashed mattress out of the window.

A middle-aged man had come across a tool box. He was stuffing all his pockets, pressed a brand new hammer into my hand.

a) *What impression do you get of the woman?*
b) *Why were these ordinary people behaving like this?*
c) *What did the boy do with the hammer?*

17 There was such power and authority in the stranger's voice that Hans began to climb into his overcoat without a murmur. Somehow, he no longer doubted his visitors' credentials and never thought of asking for any proof. He was worried, but not yet seriously alarmed. Of course, it was obvious what had happened. He remembered hearing about a science-fiction writer during the war who had described the atom bomb with disconcerting accuracy. When so much secret research was going on, such accidents were bound to occur. He wondered just what it was he had given away.

At the doorway, he looked back into his workshop and at the men who were following him.

'It's all a ridiculous mistake,' he said. 'If I *did* show anything secret in the programme, it was just a coincidence. I've never done anything to annoy the F.B.I.'

It was then that the second man spoke at last, in very bad English and with a most peculiar accent.

'What is the F.B.I.?' he asked.

But Hans didn't hear him.

The story ends with just one sentence. Have a guess at what it is.

18 And I changed him into a wheelbarrow there and then – a bright red metal wheelbarrow with a pneumatic tyre.

The class went suddenly quiet, the way they do when you take a strong line, and during the next half-hour, we got a lot of work done. When the bell for morning break went I drove them all out so as to have the room to myself.

'All right, Thomis,' I said. 'You can change back now.'

Nothing happened.

So what did the teacher do?

19 On Saturday I remarked to my husband, 'Do you think kindergarten is too unsettling for Laurie? All this toughness and bad grammar, and this Charles boy sounds like such a bad influence.'

'It'll be all right,' my husband said reassuringly. 'Bound to be people like Charles in the world. Might as well meet them now as later.'

On Monday Laurie came home late, full of news. 'Charles,' he shouted as he came up the hill; I was waiting anxiously on the front steps, 'Charles,' Laurie yelled all the way up the hill, 'Charles was bad again.'

'Come right in,' I said, as soon as he came close enough. 'Lunch is waiting.'

'You know what Charles did?' he demanded, following me through the door. 'Charles yelled so in school they sent a boy in from first grade to tell the teacher she had to make Charles keep quiet, and so Charles had to stay after school. And so all the children stayed to watch him.'

'What did he do?' I asked.

'He just sat there,' Laurie said, climbing into his chair at the table. 'Hi Pop, y'old dust mop.'

'Charles had to stay after school today,' I told my husband. 'Everyone stayed with him.'

'What does this Charles look like?' my husband asked Laurie. 'What's his other name?'

'He's bigger than me,' Laurie said. 'And he doesn't have any rubbers and he doesn't ever wear a jacket.'

Monday night was the first Parent–Teachers meeting, and only the fact that Jannie had a cold kept me from going; I wanted passionately to meet Charles's mother. On Tuesday Laurie remarked suddenly, 'Our teacher had a friend come see her in school today.'

'Charles's mother?' my husband and I asked simultaneously.

'Naaah,' Laurie said scornfully. 'It was a man who came and made us do exercises. Look.' He climbed down from his chair and squatted down and touched his toes. 'Like this,' he said. He got solemnly back into his chair and said, picking up his fork, 'Charles didn't even *do* exercises.'

'That's fine,' I said heartily. 'Didn't Charles want to do exercises?'

'Naaah,' Laurie said. 'Charles was so fresh to the teacher's friend he wasn't *let* do exercises.'

'Fresh again?' I said.

'He kicked the teacher's friend,' Laurie said. 'The teacher's friend told Charles to touch his toes like I just did and Charles kicked him.'

'What are they going to do about Charles, do you suppose?' Laurie's father asked him.

Laurie shrugged elaborately. 'Throw him out of the school, I guess,' he said.

Wednesday and Thursday were routine; Charles yelled during story hour and hit a boy in the stomach and made him cry. On Friday Charles stayed after school again and so did all the other children.

With the third week of kindergarten Charles was an institution in our family; Jannie was being a Charles when she cried all afternoon; Laurie did a Charles when he filled his wagon full of mud and pulled it through the kitchen; even my husband, when he caught his elbow in the telephone cord and pulled telephone, ash tray, and a bowl of flowers off the table, said, after the first minute, 'Looks like Charles.'

a) *How do you think things went during the third and fourth weeks?*
b) *Did Charles continue to misbehave?*

20 'Ladies and gentlemen,' called the blonde announcer, putting away the revolver, 'that concludes the performance.'

I couldn't believe it.

I exchanged one last look with the lion as the curtain was drawn across the stage. I even clapped feebly with the others. And the next thing I was outside.

'Look!' shouted Harry Finch. 'That shaggy 'un – I knocked it off.' He dangled an enormous coconut before my eyes.

'Black peas an' roasted spuds,' sighed Basher. 'Here' – he grabbed my head and pressed my ear against his fat, warm stomach – 'can you hear 'em churning about inside? Luv'ly.'

Harry shook the coconut against my ear. 'Fair loaded with milk. I knocked it clean off with the last ball. A right good tanner's worth.'

'Not as good as mine,' said Basher. 'First I had a plate of hot peas, then a bag of roasted spuds, an' then another plate of hot peas.'

The image of old Nero seemed fastened before my eyes; the smell of the lion, the sleepy old head, and gentle blinking eyes. *The fiercest lion in captivity.* We went walking along the streets homeward.

'How was the lion-taming show?' they asked at last.

How did he reply?

21 The Schneiders' door dangled from a hinge. The glass had splintered from its frame.

In the kitchen Frau Schneider lay on the floor, her lips blue, her breathing laboured.

Friedrich had a lump the size of a fist on his forehead. He bent over his mother, talking to her in a whisper. He didn't notice me.

A man stepped across Frau Schneider's legs without looking down. He emptied a large box of silver cutlery out of the window.

In the living room a woman was smashing china plates. 'Meissen!' she said proudly, when she noticed me.

Another woman was slashing every picture in the room with Herr Schneider's letter opener.

A dark-haired giant stood by Herr Schneider's bookcase. He took one volume after another from the shelves. He gripped each book by its binding and tore it apart in the middle. 'Bet you can't do the same!' he boasted with a laugh.

In Friedrich's room a man was trying to push the whole bedframe through the window. 'Come and help!' he invited me.

a) *How did the boy feel about what he saw?*
b) *What did he do next?*

22 So he sat down and began to draw.

Even if the producer of Captain Zipp had not lost patience with his set designer, Hans Muller's ideas would certainly have made him sit up and take notice. There was an authenticity and realism about them that made them quite outstanding. They were completely free from the element of phonyness that had begun to upset even Captain Zipp's most juvenile followers. Hans was hired on the spot.

He made his own conditions, however. What he was doing he did largely for love, notwithstanding the fact that it was earning him more money than anything he had ever done before in his life. He would take no assistants, and would remain in his little workshop. All that he wanted to do was to produce the prototypes, the basic designs. The mass production could be done somewhere else – he was a craftsman, not a factory.

The arrangement had worked well. Over the last six months Captain Zipp had been transformed and was now the despair of all the rival space operators. This, his viewers thought, was not just a serial about the future. It *was* the future – there was no argument about it. Even the actors seemed to have been inspired by their new surroundings: off the set, they sometimes behaved like twentieth-century time travellers stranded in the Victorian Age, indignant because they no longer had access to the gadgets that had always been part of their lives.

But Hans knew nothing about this. He toiled away happily, refusing to see anyone except the producer, doing all his business over the telephone – and watching the final result to ensure that his ideas had not been mutilated. The only sign of his connection with the slightly fantastic world of commercial TV was a crate of Crunche in one corner of the workshop. He had sampled one mouthful of this present from the grateful sponsor and had then remembered thankfully that, after all, he was not paid to eat the stuff.

He was working late one Sunday evening, putting the final touches to a new design for a space helmet, when he suddenly realized that he was no longer alone.

a) *How do you think Hans felt about this?*
b) *If you had been Hans, what would you have done?*
c) *What do you think Hans did?*

---

23   He stared at me in a glazed sort of way for a moment and then made a violent effort to concentrate.

'It's Teddy's teacher,' he bawled to those inside. 'You're just in time. Come in and have a spot of something.'

'Well, actually,' I said, 'I've come about Teddy . . .'

'It can wait,' said Mr Thomis. 'Come on in.'

'No, but it's serious,' I said. 'You see, I turned Teddy into a wheelbarrow this morning, and now . . .'

'Come and have a drink first,' he said urgently.

So I went in, and drank to the healths of Mr and Mrs Thomis. 'How much did you win?' I asked politely.

'Eleven thousand quid,' said Mr Thomis. 'What a lark, eh?'

'And now,' I said firmly, 'about Teddy.'

'Oh, this wheelbarrow caper,' said Mr Thomis. 'We'll soon see about that.'

He dragged me outside into the yard and went up to the wheelbar-row. 'Is this him?' he said.
  I nodded.

a) *What did Mr Thomis do?*
b) *What happened next?*

---

24 'We don't have any Charles in the kindergarten.'

So what had been happening?

---

25 I felt hands tugging me back by the jacket. 'Hy, where are you off?' asked Basher.
  'Quick,' I said, 'let's get in afore the crowd.'
  'What crowd?' asked Harry.
  'One small coin, ladies and gentlemen, sixpence only, brings you the greatest thrill of all time!'
  'Keep still,' hissed Basher.
  'Get your tanners ready,' I said, 'we can't afford to miss it.'
  'No, you don't,' said Basher. 'Black peas, a whacking great plateful for tuppence, an' finish off with roasted spuds.'
  'Big hairy coconuts,' whispered Harry.
  I couldn't take my eyes off Waldo, unsmiling and unafraid. He bowed to us, stepped from the platform, and disappeared.

What did the storyteller do?

26 At first I just played with the hammer. Without paying attention I swung it loosely from my wrist, back and forth, back and forth. At one point I must have nicked something – glass crashed at my blow.

a) *How did he feel about that?*
b) *What did he do next?*

27 'I'm sorry,' continued the intruder. 'But there has been a serious leak. It may be – uh – accidental, even unconscious, but that does not affect the issue. We will have to investigate you. Please come with us.'

Where do you think they were taking Hans?

28 I thought at first he was sulking, but after a while I began to think that something had gone seriously wrong. I went round to the Head-master's office.

'Look,' I said, 'I just changed Thomis into a wheelbarrow and I can't get him back.'

'Oh,' said the Head and stared at the scattering of paper on his desk. 'Are you in a violent hurry about it?'

'No,' I said. 'It's a bit worrying, though.'

'Which is Thomis?'

'Scruffy little fellow – pasty-faced – always got a sniff and a mouthful of gum.'

'Red hair?'

'No, that's Sanderson. Black, and like a bird's nest.'

'Oh yes. I've got him. Well, now,' he looked at the clock. 'Suppose you bring this Thomis chap along here in about half an hour?'

'All right,' I said.

I was a bit thoughtful as I went upstairs to the Staff Room. Tongelow was brewing the tea, and as I looked at him I remembered that he had some sort of official position in the Union.

'How would it be if I paid my Union sub?' I said.

He put the teapot down gently. 'What've you done?' he asked. 'Pushed a kid out of a second-floor window?'

I pretended to be hurt. 'I just thought it was about time I paid,' I said. 'It doesn't do to get too much in arrears.'

In the end he took the money and gave me a receipt, and when I had tucked that away in my wallet I felt a lot better.

Back in my own room Thomis was still leaning up in his chair, red and awkward, a constant reproach to me. I could not start any serious work, so after about ten minutes I set the class something to keep them busy and then lifted Thomis down and wheeled him round to the Head.

What do you think the headmaster did?

---

29   'You know what Charles did today?' Laurie demanded at the lunch table, in a voice slightly awed. 'He told a little girl to say a word and she said it and the teacher washed her mouth out with soap and Charles laughed.'

'What word?' his father asked unwisely, and Laurie said, 'I'll have to whisper it to you, it's so bad.' He got down off his chair and went around to his father. His father bent his head down and Laurie whispered joyfully. His father's eyes widened.

'Did Charles tell the little girl to say *that*?' he asked respectfully.

'She said it *twice*,' Laurie said. 'Charles told her to say it *twice*.'

'What happened to Charles?' my husband asked.

'Nothing,' Laurie said. 'He was passing out the crayons.'

Monday morning Charles abandoned the little girl and said the evil word himself three or four times, getting his mouth washed out with soap each time. He also threw chalk.

My husband came to the door with me that evening as I set out for the PTA meeting. 'Invite her over for a cup of tea after the meeting,' he said. 'I want to get a look at her.'

'If only she's there,' I said prayerfully.

'She'll be there,' my husband said. 'I don't see how they could hold a PTA meeting without Charles's mother.'

What do you think happened at the PTA meeting?

30 'Champion,' I said. 'Worth anybody's money.'

'You've not had much to say about it,' remarked Harry, suspiciously.

'Yes, you've kept your trap shut,' accused Basher.

'It were that exciting,' I said, 'as it took my breath away.'

'Something did,' they said.

I longed to tell them, to unload the misery of my heart, but I dared not. I'd never have lived it down if I had.

'Sorry, lads,' I said, 'but I've got to be in early.' And I ran off home.

I slept badly that night. Next morning when I was on my way to school Harry Finch called out, 'He's here, Mum!'

'What's up?' I asked.

'Haven't you heard?' he said.

'Heard what?' I said.

'Waldo the Lion-tamer has been badly mauled by that wild lion. It's on the front page of the *Dispatch*. I told me mum an' she wants to ask you about it.'

Out came Mrs Finch with her spectacles on and the *Dispatch* in her hand. 'Ee luv, they say he's in a critical condition –'

'Let's have a look, please,' I said to Mrs Finch. It was true. The lion had mauled him! I gave her the paper back.

What do you think he said?

---

31 Other men from the group joined in. At first singly, then in unison, they threw themselves against the door of the building.

Even the women leaped to their aid.

Only the woman who had been so abusive earlier stayed where she was; she cheered the others on.

Soon her 'one–two–three–one–two–three!' resounded through the street.

And in the rhythm of her shouts, men and women hurled themselves against the door.

From the circle of bystanders more and more joined in. Egged on by the woman, they gradually joined her chant. It was then that I caught myself shouting 'one–two–three' and edging closer with each shout. All at once I, too, was straining at the door and didn't know how I had got there. I also noticed that no one was watching now.

All took part.

Very slowly the door gave way. When it finally burst open, no one expected it. Those in the first row fell into the house. The ones behind them stumbled across the wreckage. The rest crowded in after.

a) *Why did the boy join in the shouting?*
b) *Why was no one watching any more?*
c) *What did they all do once they were inside the building?*

32 He had just seen the space-ship.

33 '. . . you're too soft with the kids. Here, come in and have another drink.'

34 His face was all powdered, and there was a smell of stale beer off him. He looked at us with disgust. And then the announcer bustled in. The curtain was pulled open, and there was a cage. Lying in the nearest corner was a big lion. It was less than a yard away from me, and it blinked its eyes and gave a good-tempered yawn.

'During the act, ladies and gentlemen, there must be complete silence. One sound, and Waldo may never come out alive. His life is in your hands. Since no insurance company will insure Waldo's life, I ask any of you who can afford it to place an extra coin in the hat. Thank you!'

Waldo cracked his whip outside the cage, and Nero slowly got to his feet. The woman took a revolver out of her pocket. Waldo went to the door of the cage, and sprang back when the lion came. This seemed to disturb the lion. As it moved away Waldo quickly opened the cage and darted inside. He cracked the whip, and Nero loped wearily round the cage. He went after it, cracking the whip over his head. *'Silence!'* called the announcer. Nero skipped round the cage for about two minutes, then sank down to rest in the same corner. Waldo leapt to the door, opened it, and got out. Nero never moved. It looked at me again, blinked, sighed, and rested.

a) *How did the boy feel about what he had seen?*
b) *What sort of a time do you think Basher and Harry had been having?*

35

I slunk downstairs again.

Mother was peering through a crack in the door, trembling. Fearfully, she pulled me into the flat. She pushed me into our living room.

We stood by the window and looked down on the street. Above us the crashing and tramping continued.

'Jew, kick the bucket!' a woman screeched outside. It was our newspaper lady.

An armchair rushed past our window and thudded into the rosebushes in our front garden.

Mother began to weep loudly.

I wept with her.

36

He was on his knees on the carpet, jacket and tie off, with sweat pouring off his face. He got up weakly when he saw me.

'I've tried everything,' he said, 'and I can't budge him. Did you do anything unorthodox?'

'No,' I said. 'It was only a routine punishment.'

'I think you'd better ring the Union,' he said. 'Ask for Legal Aid – Maxstein's the lawyer – and see where you stand.'

'Do you mean we're stuck with this?' I said.

'You are,' said the Head. 'I should ring now, before they go to lunch.'

I got through to the Union in about ten minutes and luckily Maxstein was still there. He listened to my story, grunting now and then.

'You are a member, I suppose?'

'Oh yes,' I said.

'Paid up?'

'Certainly.'

'Good,' he said. 'Now let me see. I think I'd better ring you back in an hour or so. I've not had a case quite like this before, so I'll need to think about it.'

'Can't you give me a rough idea of how I stand?' I said.

'We're right behind you, of course,' said Maxstein. 'Free legal aid and all the rest of it. But . . . but I don't fancy your chances,' he said and rang off.

The afternoon dragged on, but there was no phone call from Maxstein. The Head got fed up with Thomis and had him wheeled out into the passage. At break-time I phoned the Union again.

'Sorry I didn't ring you,' said Maxstein when I got through to him again. I've been very busy.'

'What am I to do?' I asked.

'The whole thing,' said Maxstein, 'turns on the attitude of the parents. If they decide to prosecute I'll have to come down and work out some line of defence with you.'

'Meanwhile,' I said, 'Thomis is still a wheelbarrow.'

'Quite. Now here's what I suggest. Take him home tonight – yourself. See his people and try to get some idea of their attitude. You never know; they might be grateful.'

'Grateful?' I said.

'Well, there was that case in Glasgow – kid turned into a mincing machine – and the mother was as pleased as could be and refused to have him changed back. So go round and see, and let me know in the morning.'

'All right,' I said.

At 4 o'clock I waited behind and then, when the place was empty, wheeled Thomis out into the street.

I attracted quite a lot of attention on the way, from which I guessed the story must have preceded me. A lot of people I did not know nodded or said, 'Good evening,' and three or four ran out of shops to stare.

At last I reached the place and Mr Thomis opened the door. The house seemed to be full of people and noise, so I gathered it was a party in celebration of the Pools.

a) *How did Mr Thomis receive the teacher?*

b) *What happened?*